#HouseHack

Justin La Favor

(with Sandra Umrysh)

LEGAL DISCLAIMER AND LAWYER'ESQUE MOUSE-PRINT:

Be smart. Do your homework. Plan for the future.
And at all times, take responsibility for your life and your decisions.

The Author (Justin La Favor, and Co-Author Sandra Umrysh) are Licensed Real Estate Associates in the Province of Alberta, and at the time of publication of this book, hold said real estate license(s) at MaxWell Challenge Realty (Brokerage of Record). 201-6650 177 Street NW, Edmonton AB T5T 4J5 (780-483-4848).

Stories & experiences in this book are provided voluntarily, with no compensation received by clients/those interviewed. For privacy, names of third-party individuals are modified. But in all cases, these are real people and, with only two exceptions (James & G.Yeezy) are their actual names and their actual HouseHack experiences.

DEDICATION

To All Those Dedicated To Achieving More.

Let's Go Make It Happen!

#GetEMPOWERED

CONTENTS

ACKNOWLEDGMENTS

* i *

This book wouldn't be possible without the individuals profiled within being open to sharing their stories about their #HouseHack experiences.

And none of those stories would've been possible without their trust in me to help them reach their real estate goals. This trust, and the relationships with these fantastic human beings, and really ALL of the folks that make up the "EMPOWER Family" is something I value above any "deal" that any outsider may think a real estate professional would be motivated by.

Thank YOU #EmpowerFamily for your trust, your support, your kind words on social media, and for passing along the referral of your friends and family…Which is the highest trust and compliment that we can receive.

Love you ALL with ALL my heart.

* ii *

Thank you especially to my wife, Kate, for believing in me no matter what the economy or the housing market does. For always encouraging me. And for taking care of the crazy schedules with our kids so I can give 100% to EMPOWER Clients all the time. None of this is possible without you. Any client reading this owes YOU a huge debt of gratitude.   xoxoxo

* iii *

Extra Special mention to my broker/manager Gary Zimmel at MaxWell Challenge Realty. I wouldn't be where I am, EMPOWER wouldn't exist, if it weren't for your support over the years. You really do know "What's Going On" despite the decades long-running joke you pull everyday at the office. (If you're a real estate agent in Edmonton, AB or looking to become one, you'd be an absolute idiot to not call Gary for a meeting).

* iv *

Lastly, a two-fold shoutout here, first to Gary Riz! Your graphics work on the books I've written (and continue to publish) is always stellar. And you are always SO gracious about last-minute revisions and creative input from my non-technical self. Second, to Walter Perez. For introducing me to G.Riz, and for encouraging me years ago to write books and become "more" than "just a real estate dude…" #BreakThrough!

WELCOME TO THE "HOUSE HACK NATION"

All across the continent, more and more pragmatic individuals are joining the ranks of savvy first-time buyers in executing the House Hack strategy.

But as you'll see from more than a few examples in this book, you don't have to be a first-time buyer, or a Millennial, to benefit from the power of the House Hack.

In this short book, you're going to read about the stories and examples of people just like you who have done exactly what we promise to show you: How to purchase an owner-occupied property for yourself that has the potential to generate income for you to subsidize the cost of ownership, or cover your expenses, or save for financial stability and protect yourself from job loss, or to pay for your travels around the world.

Like the title says, this is a way to "hack" your house so it can serve multiple purposes (put a roof over your head, WHILE creating an opportunity for you to make some money), instead of just causing you to spend money while you pay for the entire costs of ownership (mortgage, taxes, utilities, insurance, maintenance, etc).

"Hacking" your house so you can create an extra $250, $400, $700, or even $1000+ every month allows you to make use of an additional $3000, $4800, $8400 or $12,000 every year that you otherwise wouldn't have had before!

(Imagine This for a Second: If your gross income for last year amounted to $60,000...Then generating an extra $500 per month is like giving yourself a raise of 10%! Try finding a boss who will give you a 10% raise out of thin air for virtually minimal extra effort at your current job, especially in THIS economy!).

In other booming metropolitan areas, the House Hack strategy has the potential to reward you with even greater financial gain. Just take a quick look on any online classified site for real estate rental listings in cities like New York, San Francisco, Vancouver, Toronto, Los Angeles: People are paying a FORTUNE for the privilege of calling these places home.

In many urban areas, renters are willing to pay a

disproportionate amount of their monthly take-home pay for even the smallest of rental apartments. Some of these places are so small, that renters in 90% of other markets wouldn't even consider them a place to call home, and would refer to them as a "closet". (Heck, I grew up with a fellow who saved piles of money while going to college by paying only $300/month to rent the large closet off the kitchen in his friend's condo. Literally, a pantry/walk-in closet.)

The above example might be a bit extreme, but it doesn't take a lot of searching on Google to find headlines that talk about the growing need for affordable housing in urban areas.

This presents a profound opportunity for the would-be home buyer who is flexible in their thinking, and open to an often overlooked living arrangement of providing a place for a roommate or renter to stay, in exchange for very affordable compensation to You, the home owner.

And the best part is: You don't have to do anything different than you'd already be doing had you just bought any old place to call home. But if you do it with a certain PERSPECTIVE in mind, (that of intending to buy a home you can "hack"), this "found money" is yours for the claiming...You've just got to pull the trigger and make it happen!.

This Is A Blank Page.

Feel Free To Make Notes…

…Or Doodle.

JAMES AND THE GIANT IDEA

It was one of those days where the Mercury drops below -31 degrees…

It gets pretty cold and snowy during the Canadian winter months where I'm from here in Edmonton, Alberta.

Undeterred by the weather of the day, I had the pleasure of taking out a buyer, we'll call him James*, to view some properties that he was considering for his first ever home.

James is a plumber, owned his own plumbing company at the time, and is smart with his money. So naturally, when we started talking about secondary suites and income potential, his ears perked up when I started telling stories about clients who purchased homes without secondary suites at all…But were still pulling in **thousands** of dollars every year into their pocket!

He wanted to know more. And we both wanted to get a warm double-double at Tim's before our next viewing, so off we went in search of liquid-Canuck-warmth while I continued telling James how he could benefit from receiving income from real estate WITHOUT having to purchase an entirely separate rental property.

I'd imagine because YOU are reading THIS book NOW, that you too want to discover how others have done the same.

I've been sitting on this book for a few years now, never taking the time to put pen to paper, or pick up the phone to schedule interviews with my past clients who have done or are doing this as you read these words.

But the time is *now*.

With government policy driving up the cost of living, people are looking for ways to make ends meet. (And while I won't get into discussing political ideology in these pages, let me say that REGARDLESS of what government is in power, inflation and currency devaluation by central banks are eating away at your purchasing power. Every. Single. Year. But we'll save the critiques of fractional-reserve banking for another time.)

It doesn't really matter who's running the government

at the end of the day, and waiting for "the other guy or gal" to get into office is just wasting time. **Time that you could be taking advantage of.**

Because the fact is that the cost of living is going up world wide. YOU don't have to be a victim of rising costs though. YOU don't need to be left behind financially and economically...unless you choose NOT to do something about it.

James wanted to know more about this concept of "House Hacking".

We talk about "Life Hacks" all the time. There's productivity hacks. Smart-phone app hacks. Diet hacks to get you trimmer and slimmer.

Luminaries like Tim Ferriss have written books and built entire careers around the concept of "hacks". Just look at his recent book "Tools of Titans" or his first effort "The 4-Hour Work Week".

Hacks to maximizing the benefits you receive in life are everywhere. You maybe see the articles on your social media feed every morning when you're scrolling through your smart phone when you should be heading to work or school on-time (Com'on. Admit it. You do it too...)

There's whole sections of books and websites and blogs dedicated to showing people the "short cuts" and "hacks" to repurposing one thing and raising its value by altering its use, or multiplying its effectiveness at said-use.

And with this book, we're going to talk about exactly what we mean by "House Hack", show you examples of other people who have already done it and are continuing to do it, and how you can do it too.

THE GIANT IDEA:
**Taking your existing (or future) residence and by changing how you view it, shifting it from "costing" you money…
…to MAKING you money.**

"House Hack" means to get yourself into a piece of real estate that you own and occupy (and CAN AFFORD) yourself, BUT with additional extra space that you can use to rent out.

This is quite different than a typical "income property" where you're buying an entirely different property altogether apart from your principal residence. While I'm an advocate of owning rental properties outside your own principal residence, I'll be the first to caution someone who has concerns about managing and maintaining an additional property: If you don't know how you're going to be able to pay for a second property if it sits vacant for three months, then definitely that's a strategy you'll want to plan out carefully and only attempt with the right guidance .

(Shameless plug and shout-out to fellow Robert Graham enthusiast Don Campbell and his fine team over at REIN if rental properties are your aim. Not only does he rock a splendid hair cut to go with his epic shirt collection, I highly respect him as a person and as a brilliant strategist in the area of building a solid rental real estate portfolio. "Knowledge, Wisdom, Truth" my friend! Learn more about Don by visiting his website www.DonRCampbell.com*).*

But with the House Hack, you don't need to worry about who's going to pay the bills on the property: You Will!   It's your house after all.   If you weren't generating additional income from your home, you'd still have to pay the mortgage, insurance, utilities, taxes, and maintenance, right?

Let's be 1,000% crystal clear here: What we're NOT advocating is buying a property that you COULDN'T afford without additional income from the House Hack strategy.   But why should you pay for ALL the bills when you can enlist the help of other people, who in turn receive great benefit from being able to have the use of affordable living space, for an affordable amount that's a lot less than renting an entire place by themselves? People who now don't need to go in debt with a mortgage or worry about paying all the costs of owning a piece of real estate on their own?

There are many reasons why it absolutely makes sense to forgo being tied to a mortgage on a property and rent instead of own. I talk about this in another book

I've written for home buyers ("The Better Buyer", 2012. Buy it on Amazon): If you're looking to change jobs, or move to another city in 1-2 years, or you're in a volatile industry where your income COULD drop (to throw you a curve-ball, there's a House Hack story later on about a sharp buyer who had exactly that happen to him, by the way)...Then it might make PERFECT sense for you to rent instead of own.

And if it makes sense for many people to rent instead of own, then those people are going to need a place to live.

But if it makes sense for YOU to own instead of rent (you want to build equity and wealth for YOU instead of paying off someone else's mortgage, and you're staying in the area for 3-5+ years), then I submit that it may be an interesting notion for you to consider how you can stack the deck of life in your favour, get ahead financially, and build wealth, equity, and future financial security while **doing something that you're going to do anyways** (own a home)...And hack your execution of that plan by serving the growing need that renters have for an affordable place to live.

HOW TO "HACK YOUR HOUSE": If you're looking to purchase a home, whether it's your next place or your very first place (And ESPECIALLY if it's your very first place!), consider making an investment in a property that has EXTRA SPACE that you can market and attract a renter/tenant/roommate for (we'll use these terms interchangeably in this book).

Now, unless you find a property with a secondary suite (that is, an entirely self-contained dwelling apart from the main living space of the property), we're essentially talking about getting an extra bedroom (or two, or more) and renting that out to people you screen and select to live with you. And in turn, they not only get the privilege of having a great space to call home, they also are likely saving a lot of money by paying you a fraction of what they'd have to pay if they rented an entire apartment or house all on their own.

However, if your budget DOES allow you to purchase a home with a secondary suite (or depending on the area you live in, a tri-plex or four-plex even), then that's absolutely fantastic. But many of these properties are sought after by investors with bigger, deeper pockets than the typical first-time buyer. The Case-Studies section does have an stunning example of a buyer who found success with owning a principal residence with a secondary suite...And leveraged it into multiple rentals. But don't be discouraged if your budget doesn't get you into that type of property at the moment. You can still succeed with the house Hack by getting a property with extra room(s) even if it doesn't have a second separate living space. The MAJORITY of people who succeed with the House Hack are doing so with this very same strategy.

You can too.

WHERE DID THIS IDEA COME FROM?: The idea of the "House Hack" really isn't a new one at all. My family came over from the Philippines back in the 1970's and stayed with relatives while they got settled and started a new life in a new country. For many immigrants coming from other countries, their cultural norms have multiple generations of one family living under the same roof. And when they come to a new country, it's not uncommon to find the parents and the children living in the home, along with extended family (aunts and uncles) or elders (grandparents) also living in the same home. All working. All saving their money. All pooling their resources to get ahead faster.

And it's not just Filipino culture. This is common in many other cultures across the world, whether it's Asia or India or Africa or Europe. (Go back far enough in your own family tree, and it's VERY likely that you're only a couple branches away on the family tree from a generation that did just this!)

Our own culture in North America places a high value on the ideas of "independence" and "self direction" and "autonomy", which can somewhat discourage this practice of House Hacking. When you're striking out on your own, you don't "want any help" from mom and dad. Or if you are a proud parent, perhaps you think you don't "need our kids to pay any bills".

For sure, there's nothing wrong with wanting to do

things on your own steam. But whether it's family, or it's a close friend or co-worker or someone else you like and trust, that's renting from you, there's ZERO shame in making a mutual exchange of value between you both. (In fact, with property prices fast rising out of reach in Canadian markets like Vancouver and Toronto, or in exorbitantly expensive mega-cities like New York, San Francisco, or Los Angeles, this is the ONLY way many younger or first-time buyers would be able to afford getting onto the property ladder. Is your PRIDE the only thing stopping you from making a PRAGMATIC decision that benefits your finances, your family, and your future?)

Is this really such a difficult idea?:

> *"You pay me less than it would cost you to rent your own place, and I'll share most of the space in my home with you and make sure to maintain the privacy of your own bedroom/private space. I make some money. You save some money. We both have a place to live. It's Win-Win all around..."*

Not rocket science.

But given the many financial benefits of doing so, I'm still puzzled why more home buyers (especially first time home buyers: Millennials, that's you!) don't consider the concept.

THE CAVEAT: Now, I know, there's going to be

people out there who think this is a bad idea. "I'm a very private person. I wouldn't want someone in my space..." Or "I don't like sharing..." (So valid!) Or maybe you're looking to start a family, or already have one, and the thought of "some stranger" encroaching on your dreams of the white-picket-fenced yard where your kids run and play isn't very appealing.

Those are perfectly reasonable objections.

And if that's you, then this book and the strategies herein might not be for you, Dear Home Buyer. (If that's the case, and you'd prefer to just find the right place to call home without these House Hack shenanigans, and you're in the capital region in Alberta, we'd be absolutely happy to still find you a place to call home, that's ALL your own. Just drop us a line at Justin@EmpowerRealEstateGroup.com to schedule a no-obligation Initial Consultation where we can discuss if there's a good fit to help you reach your goals. If you're living in another North American city, enter your details at Consult.HouseHackBook.com and we'll put you in touch with a real estate professional in your town or city that understands these concepts and can help you WIN with real estate like we do with our clients locally).

Before we go any further, I will make this important point right now: If you're in a relationship and your spouse or husband or wife or fiancée isn't on board with this plan, it's probably best not to push the matter unless you want to strain your relationship. Admittedly, I've even had to deal with this challenge myself. (Yes, my own "House Hack" story is in this book. And I'll say right now, my wife is a SAINT for staying married to me and putting up with living with an entrepreneur! And while she appreciated the extra income that house hacking provided for us when our family was just starting out, as we grew and had more children, it became less and less important to have extra money coming in and more and more important to have space to call our own, entirely. And I can't blame her, as our family grew, I felt the same way too!).

So if that's you, or your spouse, and the idea of sharing living space and accommodation with a room mate or tenant who's helping you buy your home and pay your mortgage isn't appealing to you, that's absolutely acceptable. Pass this book on to someone who'll appreciate it and we can see if this will help them instead. NO judgement. :-)

As I was telling James some of the stories you'll read in these pages, there were a few points that should be mentioned before we dive into the examples. On to the next chapter, shall we?...

*James is not his real name. But it's close. And he is a real person. In fact, here's a picture of him after he got keys to his very first place - A townhouse in west Edmonton. (In case James' parents read this, the bottles I got him that he's holding are TOTALLY just some fruit juice. I swear...). He's since gotten married, bought another home through me, and keeps his townhouse as a stand-alone income property now.

"James"

"Friend-Of-James"

"FRUIT JUICE"

"FRUIT JUICE"

Above: James with a friend on Closing Day. Not the same friend who ended up renting one of two extra rooms from him. Just a guy that got guilted into moving a couch.

HOW TO HOUSE HACK AND NOT GET SCREWED

First off, and this is really important and so many would-be home buyers forget this point:

**It is _YOU_ who gets to choose who
you end up renting space to and living with!**

It needs to be someone you get along with. Someone whose habits you're aware of (or know you can get accustomed to). It shouldn't be someone you don't trust. If you can't leave $20.58 in cash on your kitchen counter around this person, then they shouldn't be living under the same roof with you. **Period**.

Do NOT make the mistake of making a financial decision based on need...At the expense of a prudent decision based on wisdom. If you don't like them, or can't trust them, they shouldn't be in your home. End of story.

Secondly, make sure you **put any agreement you have in-writing**, have your room mate/renter sign the document, and ensure you provide a copy to them as soon as possible and document that you provided a copy (ie. Scan/email to them so there's a digital paper trail that's time-stamped).

Let's be honest...

Sometimes, what starts out as a good thing, goes downhill. Or circumstances change and when money gets involved, it can cause tension and create barriers to open communication. No need to worry about "he said/she said" drama if you're both (literally) on the same page with a written agreement spelling out what expectations are, who does what, and what the grounds are for ending the arrangement should one party not hold up their end of the bargain.

Thirdly, if you're in the process of searching for your first or next home, and you absolutely plan on executing the House Hack strategy, not only are you ensuring better re-sale and value-retention by getting a better-equipped home, you'll also save yourself a lot of hassle and inconvenience if you purchase a home with a MINIMUM of **TWO** **FULL BATHROOMS**.

If you're looking at your first place and it's going to be an apartment style condo, for instance, why go for the "1 Bedroom, 1 Bath" option when (if you can COMFORTABLY AFFORD IT WITHOUT THE

EXTRA RENTAL INCOME) you could go with a "2 Bedroom, 2 Bath" unit for a nominal amount more? If buying a house or half duplex, why not get the "3 Bedroom, 2.5 Bath" model for a similar price as the "3 Bedroom, 1.5 Bath" home?

(Unless you're Dylan M., who purchased a "2 Bedroom, 2.5 Bath" townhouse and is doing AMAZINGLY well generating income by renting out what is essentially a second master-bedroom-suite in his unique townhouse. More on his story later in the book @ pg. 57...).

Think "Expansion".

Don't just think about yourself. Expand your thinking to include the capacity to conveniently accommodate another individual.

If you've got a second full bathroom, you don't have to wait to take a shower or use the facilities when nature calls and your renter/roommate is occupying the only bathroom in the property. (If you've "gotta go", sometimes the inconvenience of waiting for someone who "takes their time" really isn't worth the extra money you get each month!).

Fourthly, and this was alluded to a few paragraphs ago, but...

UNDER NO CIRCUMSTANCES ARE YOU TO PURCHASE A HOME WHERE YOU *NEED* THE EXTRA INCOME TO BE ABLE TO AFFORD TO PAY YOUR BILLS.

This is <u>foolish</u>. (<-SUPREME understatement.)

If I could triple-underline that last part about being foolish, I would. But my MacBook doesn't have that feature...

This would be just as reckless as you buying a huge house with a jumbo mortgage on the high end of your price range and paying for it all yourself when it more than stretches your financial capabilities.

Don't stretch yourself thin and EXPECT that the additional income will allow you to live beyond your means. In order to be prudent, wise, responsible, you need to consider property that you can **COMFORTABLY AFFORD ON YOUR OWN**... Even if you didn't have any additional income from your House Hack.

The benefit of the House Hack is that you "*do what you'd typically do anyways, but tweak your perspectives and plans so you can make extra money (rent the extra space) for doing what you would've done anyways!*" (Ie. Buy a home for yourself).

For more information on how to qualify for a mortgage, and the other steps involved in purchasing your first or next home, drop me an email at Justin@EmpowerRealEstateGroup.com. We can also put you in touch with one of our trustworthy mortgage professionals. These are the same specialists that not only help our own clients, but that we trust, or have used PERSONALLY on our own real estate purchases. (Note: We do not receive compensation for referring you to them or any other professionals.)

Author with co-speakers at a recent EMPOWER Real Estate Group "Home Buying Seminar"; @Middle - Ralph Colistro, Lawyer; @Right - Shayne Beeler, OneSt Mortgages.

This is Another Blank Page.

Feel Free to Use it to Make Memories By Playing Tic-Tac-Toe with a Loved-One…

"WE INTERRUPT YOUR READING WITH A TIMELY ANNOUNCEMENT FOR YOUR BENEFIT…"

Before we jump into the "House Hack Case-Studies" section of the book, I wanted to give permission to those readers who, like me, tend to want to take immediate action when they have an idea in mind. (My client Travis L. was like this. After considering his goals for many months, he called me out of the blue and went from not even having a mortgage pre-approval in place, to viewing a handful of candidate homes, getting his financing in place, getting his offer accepted, and removing conditions on his very first home…All in a span of about two weeks!)

Now, if you're the type that wants to read an entire book cover-to-cover before taking any next steps, that's fine too. (I'm also like that, in some cases).

But if you're an Action-Taker like Travis and want to get the ball rolling…I want you to know: A) That's perfectly fine. You can get to the Case-Studies section later. It's not going anywhere. And B) Here's how you can get in touch and begin your process of discovering what the best next-steps look like for YOUR specific situation…

"The EMPOWER Process"

All good decisions are based on a solid foundation of planning, perspective, and the guidance of informed professionals that make up your "Team".

If you're located in the Capital Region in Alberta, and you're wanting to see if the EMPOWER Real Estate Group (ie. Me and my band of Consultative Real Estate Professionals) are the right fit to help you "Win With Real Estate" as we like to say, then your first step would be to schedule a No-Hassle, No-Pressure, Initial Consultation.

In order for us to help our clients to the highest level, it's important for us to get to know you (your goals, your dreams, your situation) on a personal level so we can give you personalized advice tailored to YOU.

And while we have clients like Travis L. (see his testimonial below), and many other buyers, who show up to their Consultation and end up finding their ideal home in a matter of days or weeks after we've sat down with them...

...We still firmly believe that, even if it takes many weeks or many months, viewing many properties, that this is entirely O.K.

Great decisions sometimes take a bit of time to make. And we're not here to "rush you" into a decision just to "make a sale" like so many other "sales agents" do (in the real estate industry, and in many other industries).

Make no mistake about it, selling is a big part of what we do. But our intent at EMPOWER is to sell you on the wisdom of:

- Making the BEST decision…
- Making the RIGHT choice the FIRST time…
- Avoiding expensive oversights and common mistakes that buyers make…

If you're looking for pushy sales-agents who are only concerned with viewing you as a "deal" or as "revenue" for their business…

…Then you have ZERO business calling us.

That's **NOT** how we roll.

We meet people every week in our day-to-day dealings who think they know everything, or are just in a mad rush to race into a bad decision. And frankly, those aren't the type of people that we can help…So we don't end up taking them on as clients.

But if you appreciate someone who appreciates you AS A PERSON (and not a "sale"), then what the typical EMPOWER process involves is two-fold:

1) We'll have you stop by our brokerage, and after

reviewing some mandatory information that real estate professionals are *legally obligated* to disclose to you (the nature of your relationship with a real estate professional), then we'll get into discussing your current situation, your goals, your dreams for the future, and how your next real estate move fits into those plans. (FYI: If you've been in contact with a real estate "professional" who hasn't reviewed these mandatory disclosures with you at the very earliest opportunity, then not only are they not abiding by the ethics and standards of the industry, I'd be willing to bet there's a good chance they're also the type to view you as a "sale" instead of a Human Being. But that's just one person's opinion...)

2) After we've concluded our Initial Consultation, we'll review what it looks like for you to officially sign on as a client and extend you the opportunity to have us represent you in your search for your next home, whether you're going to aim for a "House Hack" - style property...Or you just want the White-Picket-Fence all to yourself because sharing is overrated. ;-)

3) If we're on the same page, and you decide to join the EMPOWER Family and have us help you "Win with Real Estate", then the fun begins and we'll start the home-search process according to your timelines and schedule.

SO...

If that's appealing to you, and you're ready to take the next step in your journey, then shoot me an email at:

Justin@EmpowerRealEstateGroup.com

OR... Call Direct @ 780-405-5272

...And we'll get you set up to stop by the office for a chat.

(Remember, we're talking about a conversation here. You're not buying a house in the next five minutes just because you email us. We don't retain your contact info and spam the daylights out of your email or voicemail. Again, pushy-sales-tactics are not in our repertoire. In fact, what if you're entirely crazy? We need to figure that out first before we're going to invest time away from our families to take you out looking for a home. Then again, aren't we all a bit crazy? Maybe we might not be the "right kind of crazy" for you! So the Initial Consultation is a way to ensure that we're a good fit to work together. If you've read this far, there's a good chance you're likely the kind of awesome person that works well with how we serve our clients.)

Q: "BUT WHAT IF I DON'T LIVE IN/AROUND EDMONTON?"

Easy!

Visit **Consult.HouseHackBook.com** and fill out the quick information form and we'll put you in touch with a real estate professional in your area that has the same philosophy and approach to serving their clients as we do ours.

Executing the House Hack strategy requires local expertise, solid listening-skills, and an abundance of patience from your real estate professional. Things that a mere "pushy sales agent" likely doesn't possess. We'll make sure to set you up on the right path to Win with Real Estate and make sure your first (or next) home buying experience is a successful one.

A Few (Unpaid!) Comments Voluntarily Submitted by Happy Clients of the EMPOWER Real Estate Group...

(You'll see some of their stories in the Case-Studies section.)

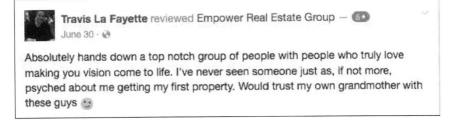

Above: Travis L. with a happy smile, and a happy future-wife (Good job, Kim, for finally getting the man to settle down!) in front of their FIRST home…And a HOUSE HACK property at that! After coming by the brokerage for an Initial Consultation, and getting hooked up with one of our top-notch mortgage specialists, Travis ended up closing on a property with a Legal Secondary Suite in the basement, and because he's a fast-action taker, he already had a tenant lined up for the basement and started collecting rent shortly after getting keys to his first place! He's since referred his sister to us, and we're honoured to be helping her reach her real estate goals as well! Great job, Travis!

Backstory: Melissa was referred to EMPOWER after her sister and brother-in-law successfully sold their half-duplex in northwest Edmonton and got a sweet deal on a beautiful bungalow in Sherwood Park. We don't just help the #HouseHackNation - When it comes to helping you "Win with Real Estate", you can count on us to give you solid perspectives and the right plan to succeed... Even if you're in a down-market, with LOTS of competition, just like Melissa.

After meeting Justin on Halloween Eve in 2014 at one of his investor-client's house-flipping projects in northeast Edmonton, Michelle was impressed by his No-Nonsense approach to serving clients with their real estate goals, as compared to the handful of other "sales agents" she had recently encountered...

> Thanks justin :) I appreciate everything. No other realtor has come close :) see you next week

…Michelle sent this text (above) shortly after meeting. And while her journey took over a year (she spent her time saving her downpayment funds before coming to an EMPOWER Client Event in Spring-2015), Michelle eventually ended up purchasing a brand-new townhouse unit with Justin's help. Though she didn't intend to rent extra bedrooms out, after an unexpected change in employment situation, Justin's previous guidance came in handy and she was able to implement the House Hack strategy to mitigate her situation. Below: Michelle & Justin having fun after removing conditions on her townhouse by Lake Summerside.

Justin's Comments: "I absolutely LOVE that Megan said 'Love' in her comments. Call it cliche, but we try to put as much love as possible into everything we do. That's why, when you're part of the EMPOWER Family, you're not 'just' a client, you're part of The Family. So glad to see that this clearly came through when we helped Megan and her husband Max sell their half-duplex for top-dollar in a crowded down-market, then turn around and get them into an amazing home in Sherwood Park!"

Backstory: After travelling around the US for Brennan's professional hockey career, he and his wife Michelle were moving back to Canada and reached out to get their home search started. You'd think that viewing homes from another country would be difficult, but we ended up previewing and compiling video tours via smart phone and sending private Facebook and DropBox links for them to review properties from out-of-country until they could come up and view them in person…

Above: Michelle & Brennan celebrating Closing Day in their beautiful new southside home with a bottle of Dom and some happy smiles!

Backstory: I met Ambur and Ryan when they called to view a beautiful two storey I had listed in Spruce Grove for Canyon Spring Homes. Despite a challenging market, we ended up selling their Edmonton two-storey (with no garage!) and helped them into this stunning customized home by the golf course in Spruce Grove.

Context: Like most of the fine folks in the EMPOWER Family, Niki and her husband Darin were referred by friends who had recently sold their acreage in the same subdivision outside of Sherwood Park after multiple other agents had tried without success. Shortly after making some adjustments to the strategy on the sale of Darin and Niki's acreage, they received multiple offers and were able to move from their acreage to a gorgeous bungalow in Sherwood Park. They've since referred Darin's parents who moved from British Columbia to Edmonton. @Below: Whatever it takes, we take care of The Family! While on vacation atop Mauna Kea volcano in Hawaii, I had the pleasure of calling Darin's father to close the deal on his new condo!

Kayla Kasteel reviewed Empower Real Estate Group — 😊
December 17, 2015 · 🌐

Admittedly when I made the choice that I was going to buy instead of rent I went into it thinking that all realtors were pushy and would try to maximize on my financial status at the time. Justin Lafavor not only showed me that was not what he was about but treated me like if I was his own daughter buying her first place as a single. He opened my eyes to different possibilities that I would have not explored on my own and it was the most relaxing purchase I have ever made which considering it was my largest is unbelievable. I write this is as I sit in my place 2 years later, with my fireplace on, and my 10 month old son, so incredibly grateful that I made the choice to trust Justin because had I gone with my original uneducated thoughts it would be a very different and sad picture.

Backstory: One of my favourite House Hack stories, Kayla is one of the hardest working and sharpest young buyers I've had the honour of helping. Discover her full House Hack story @ pg. 41 in the Case-Studies section up next…

HOUSE HACK
CASE STUDIES

(So you can get some ideas on how this
#HouseHack thing might apply to
YOUR goals…)

Sometimes I listen to music when I'm writing books...

Today, if you're catching these faintly coloured easter eggs, it's Rick Astley.

#NeverGonnaGiveYouUp...

HOUSE HACK CASE STUDIES

Kayla Kasteel

Dylan Meidinger

Sandy Umrysh

Justin's Own Story

Dan St. Pierre

"G.Yeezy"*
(*For privacy, this #HouseHack client opted for a cool pseudonym but s/he's 100% real!)

…Yes. Two pages ago, I just #RickRolled the readers of this book…

#NeverGonnaGiveNeverGonna Give!

"22 YEAR OLD SINGLE LADY BECOMES SINGLE-MOM... THEN MAKES *MORE* THAN ENDS MEET WITH HER #HOUSEHACK!"

Kayla Kasteel has been living in her condo for a number of years now, at the time of this writing. But back in January or 2017, she took some time for an interview with me about her experiences with her own #HouseHack after she received keys to her first place, a 2 bedroom 2 bath condo in Edmonton AB. The following is the Q&A session we recorded about her experience.

(Justin) *"Let's first start off with...What was it like when you first reached out to me to say 'Hey I want to get a place, let's meet up and chat...'? And what was the catalyst for your decision to OWN your own home*

***VS renting, which you'd been doing for a number of
years before we met?"***

(Kayla): The catalyst was I had a girlfriend who made
significantly less money than me, she was in retail
management, and she had bought a condo and redone
it quite nicely. Nothing super fancy. And when I went
to see her at her place, and she explained that she had
bought it for "X" amount of money and her mortgage
was about $500/month, her purchase was just over
$100k...and she had done some stuff to it, I asked
myself "What am I doing???"

At the time I was paying cheap rent, and I was like
"You're able to pull this off??" and I was making easily
3x or 4x more than she was.   At that point I was
thinking "Hey, maybe I should reevaluate my options
and look at renting and building stability instead of
paying someone else's mortgage..."

My first thoughts when I sat down with you though,
was that real estate agents, lawyers, bankers, all of those
types were people that I had a natural distrust of. Like,
I was on guard against someone who was trying to 'get
something' from me...there's so many small details and
fine print that you're not going to know about unless
you do that type of work, and that made me skeptical.

I ended up choosing you simply because of our
connection through church, I don't think I had known
anybody that had used you prior to us connecting. We
were Facebook friends and you commented on my
political posts, so there was that.... I went in skeptical,
not because of you, but because of the reputation of

"real estate" in general.

(Justin): *"It's a valid concern! ...And what were your thoughts going into that first meeting, and what were your thoughts afterwards?"*

(Kayla): When I went in, I was worried about disclosing the amount of money I was making at the time. My concern was that number would jump out at you and that would mean only the more expensive options would be presented to me... But, I do recall getting a sense of peace that you were going to work with the budget that *I* wanted to give you. Even though initially when I said I only want a $100k place, you smiled politely and said "ok"...And later it came out your reservation was more on the safety side than the money side, than anything else. You respected that, even though I could be pre-approved for closer to $400k, you were still engaging the conversation at the price point I had in mind.

And the location of our meeting was unique too...it was much more relaxing to meet in a pub environment. Probably because it wasn't your space, or my space, but more neutral ground. And I really appreciated that, instead of going to somebody's office behind closed doors and the fear of "what's going to happen?". It felt like two people meeting together for a potential opportunity VS me coming to you for a service. It felt much more mutual.

(Justin): *What was it that changed that "Skeptical"*

perspective that you initially had?"

(Kayla): After that first meeting, because I didn't feel that you were pushy…. A lot of it was a gut instinct. You didn't come across as shifty or shady or trying to upsell me or make any crazy type of promises. You got to know who I was, you understood I was a young single woman who had a father that did worry about whether I had a secured underground parking stall, even when I said it wasn't important to me, you were considering all the different elements, especially from a father's perspective, you respected what I wanted to work with financially.

(Justin): *"So let's talk about that! Your first thought was 'Debt is dumb, Cash is King, and the paid-off Toyota Echo is the new Status Symbol of today…' and you had a target budget of $100k to get a condo…"*

(Kayla): Yes, the reason for $100k was I looked at my girlfriend's one bedroom place and I thought "I could be comfortable in this". Now, she did NOT have things like underground parking, or an elevator in the building, but the rest of it was quite pleasant. One thing I did like is that when we started seeing places, and you started showing me some two bedroom options, it opened me up to the potential of a rental situation with a roommate, and I'm VERY happy I never ended up going with a one bedroom and I ended up thinking bigger than I originally planned. You showed me the things I wanted to see initially, but you also showed me what was POSSIBLE, things with potential, that I ended up choosing and I'm happy for that.

(Justin): *"Would you say you were only thinking for Immediate/Short-Term (with the one bedroom setup)?"*

(Kayla): Oh, 100%! I had $20k cash in my bank account and I thought "I might as well spend it on something worth something" instead of wasting it on more travelling...Well, I shouldn't say waste, but I had done a lot of travelling already. It wasn't like I needed to do more. When I'd see my girlfriend and saw what she had done, I was like "oh, that's doable...It's not going to stress me out or push me beyond my financial capacity."

Once I started really thinking about the two bedroom and potential opportunity going forward, and I had also had some experience with my current job, my employer was always looking for apartment rentals for newly hired staff moving to the area, I actually thought beyond that, like "When I move out of this place, what could I do with it?" I had a lot of thought to putting some nice furniture in and doing a furnished turn-key rental to corporate clientele, and it was a must in that case to have at least a two bedroom with underground parking.

So in like, one month, you had my mindset shifted quite a bit. Then I started seeing more places with you and getting more ideas.

(Justin): *"Let's touch on price differences...You ended up in a place for $207,500...Obviously a big step in price from $100k, but in terms of what you actually qualified for, where on the scale of what your lender qualified you for did you end up?"*

(Kayla): I was a green-light for almost $400k...And as you said, I ended up just over $200k, but I was still very comfortable in that price range once I saw how affordable it was to spend a little bit more and get far more space and more importantly far more potential. It didn't seem like that much of a stretch especially, well, my dad at that point had gotten involved and helped me spreadsheet the numbers and the difference in mortgage payment wasn't much, considering how much more I was getting.

I saw that and was like "Oh, ok!". In my mind, I had initially thought "well, getting a place for $100k VS $200k, my mortgage payment would be WAY more than double" but obviously that's not how it works out.

(Justin): *SIDEBAR: "When you say 'dad was involved', you didn't have any co-signer, any borrowed downpayment, no gifted downpayment from mom and dad, this was all 100% you, all the way, your own hard work & savings without any help from your parents?"*

(Kayla): That's correct. My father was involved with regards to crunching numbers and doing the math with me. I didn't even dip into my RRSP's with the first-time home buyer program, even though I had access to like $60k through that avenue. I did not even touch that money. I strictly had $20k cash in my savings account. And in my case I ended up doing 10% down.

(Justin): *"Are you okay if we share how old you are now, and how old you were when you did this? Because it's been a couple of years now..."*

(Kayla): I was 22, fresh, just turned 22 when I purchased my place. And I am 25 now. *(Ed: Interview done Jan 2017).*

(Justin): *"In terms of your blog and your financial TV show, when is THAT coming out??! Gail Vaz-Oxlade is going to be calling to do a show with you!"*

(Kayla): You know, I'll get back to you on that stuff. lol...

(Justin): *"So, on the House Hack topic, with a one bedroom, all your bills are on YOU...But with a two bedroom, you've got options, potential for roommate, potential for income, while you were moving in you said you had a couple different people renting your spare room. What was that FIRST experience like?"*

(Kayla): I had had roommate experiences in the past, so I was definitely picky with my selection, especially because it was MY home. Before, I'd pick based on

"Oh it's a friend, etc" But those aren't necessarily the people you want to choose. You want people who are consistent and reliable and responsible. You don't need to chase them for rent. So that was a huge factor for me this time around.

So "Lindsay" (*Ed: Not her girlfriend's real name*), she was a nurse, and I had met her through a coworker at work, and they were friends. So basically how I found her, is that networking is a strong suit of mine. I have many friends in many different types of social groups in life. And I just started putting out the feelers "Hey, do you know anybody for this? Here's what I'm looking for".

I didn't put out anything official like an ad, or social media, etc. I want to say it was probably a couple weeks, and then I ended up meeting Lindsay. We met for coffee and discussed some things. She was a very homebody type person, from the east coast. And we got along really well. We had very similar personalities.

Once again, a lot of it comes down to gut instinct. I knew a bunch of people she knew, and they were all stable human beings and good people. So I did go with her. I think I sat down with one other person, but I didn't go through a dozen people or anything like that.

And then, the SECOND roommate, after Lindsay moved out, "James" (*Ed: Also not his real name*), he was the son of one of my mom's best friends. We had known each other since we were both very, very, very young. And because I knew him so well, I knew a living situation would be a non-issue.

(Justin): *"So how long after you got keys did you rent to Lindsay?"*

(Kayla): I want to say that it was within a couple months after I got keys? I closed on the condo in November, and then she was moved in by January.

(Justin): *"And what was she paying and what was the setup there? Rent+Utilities split? Or All-In Flat Rate?"*

(Kayla): I chose flat-rate for sake of convenience. I wasn't home a lot at that time, working out of town. So I wasn't there to open the bills and do the math and figure that out each and every month. So I charged $700/month. That also included underground parking (I have two stalls). She got cable and internet. And that was all in one fixed-cost.

My mortgage was $960/month, so basically the majority of my mortgage was paid for by my renter and while I was saving all the income from the rent my roommates were paying, I essentially was only needing to cover a few hundred dollars in insurance, internet and cable, the condo fees, and the power bill because heat and water were included in the condo fee.

(Justin): *"That's right! I forgot your place came with TWO Underground Stalls!"*

(Kayla): Yup, and I still rent one out even though I don't have a roommate anymore after having my son.

(Justin): *"Thats so funny you view your son as an expense entry on an income statement, lol! The second stall though, that's terrific! How much are you getting?"*

(Kayla): It's only $50/month. But one thing I noticed, I was in the parkade one day, and noticed a couple guys doing some work in one of their stalls and I said "Hey, if you need some extra space, 'that stall' over there is mine, you can use it for the day if you need it." and they asked me "Well, how often is it available?" and I said "I'm actually looking to rent it out!" so they asked me "Well, How much do you want for it?"

It was pretty organic, kind of just happened. I saw somebody had a need, and ended up getting $600/year for helping them with a solution.

Honestly, if you just go about your day with the intention of helping people, and just having an awareness of what's around you, it's amazing what happens.

(Justin): *"With regards to Lindsay the nurse, how long did she stay until she moved on?"*

(Kayla): So that was January 2014...And then when James moved in, it was right back-to-back after Lindsay moved out that same year. But basically the whole calendar year, I had a renter.

(Justin): *"So roughly 11-12 months?"*

(Kayla): Yup. And with Lindsay, it wasn't that she left because we had a falling out or anything. She had a boyfriend when we first met up, and she ended up moving out of my place to move in with him when they got their own space together. And that was around the summertime. I can't recall specifically when because as I said, I was working out of town so much at the time, but I had good renters and the extra room was rented without any issues that entire year.

(Justin): *"So she's giving you $700/month, for basically having the run of your entire condo, minus your master bedroom…And was James paying the same or did you give him the Brother-From-Another-Mother discount?"*

(Kayla): Nope, it was the same deal. So again, $700/month. And I was very relaxed when it came to rules. I didn't make them sign contracts because I knew them. Technically, I'd advise getting documents signed between both parties, and I would normally do that myself in 99% of cases, but because I had pretty good pre-existing relationships with them both, I didn't feel that was necessary. I very much had a lot of trust in these people.

Once again, because I had gone through so many previous roommate situations in other places I've rented in the past, I have a pretty good feel for it. But when other people ask me my advice on the topic, I always tell them to protect themselves and get things in writing.

(Justin): *"If you went back, would you do anything differently?"*

(Kayla): So in regards to the condo, that's an interesting question. Obviously at the time, I planned for if, financially things went sideways for me, knowing the economy can change an job loss and sickness happens, I didn't anticipate getting pregnant and having my son. But it happened and I'm SO blessed. But I don't regret my place at all, however my son doesn't pay me rent, so I would've loved maybe a three bedroom place, so I could still have a renter and have that extra income.

Again, not that I need it, but having more streams of income is better than having only one. It's not like I'm struggling to put food on the table, far from it. It's just that I like to save money and my savings don't grow as fast as they would if I had that extra $8,400/year coming in from a roommate. But I absolutely love my place.

(Justin): *"So that $8,000.00+/Year, what did you put that towards?"*

(Kayla): I already had a $10k emergency fund set aside when I bought my place… In addition to my 10% downpayment. When I got all the extra money from the roommates, it didn't go into a specific account. It just went into savings.

But the big difference came was, when I was let go from my previous employer, I was 30 weeks pregnant, and obviously I wasn't expecting to have that happen. And when you're 30 weeks pregnant, it's not like you're getting another job. As much as you'd like to, and you're qualified, it just doesn't happen unfortunately. I remember that being a very frustrating point for me, because I wasn't a person that wanted handouts. But obviously that affected my finances quite a bit. I had received a big severance offer at the time, but I couldn't take it (because it was such a large amount, from all the accrued vacation and banked sick days) that, if I did take it, I wouldn't' qualify for maternity-leave.

So… My finances got a bit funny for the next year. Because of that, all the money I had gotten from renting and my emergency fund, I had that cushion for the period of time I was unable to work and get a steady paycheque, but I couldn't accept the large lump sum payout.

(Justin):   *"That's UNREAL that happened to you! How long was that period of time where you couldn't/weren't able to work?"*

(Kayla): I had ten weeks where I had nothing coming in, but then EI kicked in (for maternity) and I took about a year off. By itself, it covered my housing costs, but obviously not for having a baby and raising it. So every month I was dipping into my savings for that year. But because of the House Hack income, I had a LOT of savings to get me by!

(Justin):   *"Would it be accurate to say the money you* *received from your roommates, while you were pregnant and going through that period of time where you weren't working...Was a game-changer for making ends meet during all that drama?"*

(Kayla): Oh, 100%... Like, 100%! That extra money was KEY in making ends meet and being comfortable. I didn't have to borrow money from my folks, or go into debt, or sell something to make my mortgage payment. Obviously I didn't have the same lifestyle and spending habits as before. But the most important part was that it wasn't like I had to change things drastically or suffer because of it.

(Justin): *"WOW. That's so awesome. If you were going to give anybody any advice about their own House Hack goals, what would it be?"*

(Kayla): I'd encourage people, and I wish I had done this, treat it seriously. Interview people. Don't have it be casual thing where they come in with demands. Set your expectations and boundaries up front. And don't have a hundred rules, BUT have firm clear rules that you don't back down from.

And have some sort of contract. I was comfortable with month to month. But of course, if you're a new home owner, and you're building up that extra emergency fund, and you don't have the amount of income coming in that I had, set up fixed monthly tenancy with damage deposit etc. What I did and what I'd tell others to do, are different. I get that.

(Justin): *"Would you like to add anything?"*

(Kayla): For my whole experience, overall, how would I summarize this?… I think if you have the extra income to do so, not to stretch yourself thin using every penny to get into real estate. But if you've built up some cash reserves in your life, it IS good to buy a place that is not at your maximum. Because it gives you options.

I don't know my game plan with this place. I'm three years in. I haven't decided if I want to buy something else and use this as a rental. But at least I have options. And (*at the time of this interview*) I'm only 25, single mom, with no child support.

(Justin): *"Tell your parents I need them to write a parenting book, because I want one. Badly. They did a great job… You're a rockstar Kayla!"*

(Kayla): I don't feel like I've been shafted in life, despite some of the recent challenges I've had to overcome. A lot of people were initially like 'Oh, you poor single girl, you got let go from your job, you're pregnant, etc' and I still see myself as one of the most blessed people in this world in regards to the country I live in and the opportunities that I have. The ability to go to work. I hear there's a recession out there, and there's an evil government trying to destroy everything. But, I choose to make my own reality.

(Justin): *"Haha, that's great. Are you okay if I*

copy-paste your last comments verbatim into the book?"

(Kayla): Of course!

(Justin): *"I'm really excited for your interview. Thanks so much for sharing your story. The world needs more young adults showing what's possible when you work hard, save your money, and plan for the future. You're such a great example for others to follow. Thanks again for your time Kayla!"*

(Kayla): Absolutely. And I'll also end with this. There's so much power in curiosity. I wouldn't have known ANYTHING about home ownership unless I stopped and asked "Why? Why not me? Why not now?"

Kayla's House Hack Summary:

Property Type:
2 BR / 2 BA condo w/ x2 U/G Stalls

Purchase Price:
$207,500

Extra $ Made From #HouseHack:
$8,000+ in approx. 12 months, renting out ONE spare bedroom @ $700/month

---

"FIRST TIME HOME BUYER GETS KEYS...LOSES JOB... AND HIS #HOUSEHACK ROOMMATE PAYS HIS BILLS!"

Dylan Meidinger has a penchant for travelling. A journeyman tradesperson, his profession like many in other trades is subject to the ups and downs of the economy. So when he called me shortly after receiving keys to his townhouse to tell me the shop he was working at had let him go, I was concerned.

But he laughed and told me how the roommate he had secured was basically covering his costs. Shortly after (in a matter of weeks) he had a new position with a different shop.

And his random updates over the years illustrate why it's so powerful for unattached first-time buyers to consider joining the #HouseHack Nation. Especially with how many overseas trips this guy takes every year...*All basically paid for by his roommate tenants!*

The following is Dylan's story in his own words, both his post-move-in testimonial, as well as a more recent update during an interview conducted at one of our Client Events, a Christmas party in December 2016...

(Justin): *"So you bought a home...What were your thoughts on the process of buying, and what were you looking for?"*

(Dylan): I talked to you about buying a house a few times over a couple years. And then when I got established in my career, I had reached out to talk to you about getting my first place.

(Justin): *"What did you initially think about finding in your first home... And then how did that compare to what we actually helped you get into?"*

(Dylan): We met at your brokerage and talked about possible options. At the time, I didn't really have many ideas, so we went to see a few places.

At first I think I just was thinking about getting a condo for myself and that was it. So we went through all these different places, and the entire time, you were asking me lots of questions and taking notes about what I liked and why I liked it, and what I didn't like and why. It was really low-pressure, which was kind of nice because a lot of my friends who had bought before had said they didn't like that their agent was really pushy and high-pressure.

(Justin): *"How many places do you think we went to see?"*

(Dylan): Probably...honestly, like 30 or 40 maybe? And you took your time. I really appreciate that to this day. The funny part was, the place I'm in was one of the ones we went to see on the very first time we went out. It's the one I ended up coming back to!

(Justin): *"So what did you end up getting?"*

(Dylan): Well, it was through a builder that was developing two-storey townhouses. And they had a three-bedroom option with an ensuite and a full bathroom upstairs... And then we went to the place that had two full master-suites, basically two really big bedrooms that both had walk-in closets and full ensuite bathrooms. And I went with that because it's easy to rent out the spare bedroom, and that way I have my own master suite, and I rent the second suite out for basically half my costs (for owning my home).

(Justin): *"Are you okay to talk about those numbers? What are you charging? How long have you been there?"*

(Dylan): Four years in the spring. (*Ed: Dylan closed on his townhouse around Spring 2013*)

(Justin): *"And how long have you House Hacked and had it (your second master bedroom suite) rented in that time?"*

(Dylan): It's been only 3 or 4 months out of the last four years or so that I haven't had income from a roommate.

(Justin): *"Have you had any challenges finding anyone to rent to?"*

(Dylan): Not really... No. lol.

(Justin): *"What do you typically charge? Is it rent +utilities split, or flat-rate?"*

(Dylan): About $900/month flat rate, and I include all utilities etc.

(Justin): *"OK, so hold on, you've been there roughly four years, and apart from less than 10% vacancy you're pulling in nearly $12,000/year in EXTRA income??"*

(Dylan): Yeah man! It pays over half my mortgage. I pay $775 every two weeks so, do the math. Hahaha. I actually have my current roommate, she's moving out at the end of the month, and I've got one guy from work and then two other friends all asking if they can be the one to move in. So I'm in the process of deciding who I'd like to move in with me.

(Justin): *"You're like 'Joey' from 'Friends", "Who wants to live at Joey's?" lol. So you have no problems finding people?"*

(Dylan): None. At all.

(Justin): *"What end of town are you in?"*

(Dylan): Westend in the Hamptons. Great location.

(Justin): *"What challenges have you had?"*

(Dylan): The one time was this young guy, from Vancouver, who was moving to town. His mom was responding to ads for him and found my place. So he moves in, and four months later decided he couldn't handle living away from his parents, so he packed his bags and loaded his van and drove back to Vancouver.

(Justin): *"Apart from that, it's been cool?"*

(Dylan): For sure.

(Justin): *"If you could do anything differently, what would that be?"*

(Dylan): I don't know if I'd do anything differently to be honest.

(Justin): *"With all the money you've made from your #HouseHack, how has it helped you financially?"*

(Dylan): With the way things have been going lately in Alberta, I've worked primarily in oilfield construction, In the last year and a half I'd work for 3-4 months, get laid off, work for a bit, get laid off again. The House Hack strategy has made it so I don't have any issues or fears whatsoever. It's made it so that economic downturns, job loss, any of that sort of stuff, if I was just trying to take care of a place on my own, like if I had gone with a one bedroom condo like I originally was thinking, it'd have been a lot more stressful financially.

(Justin): *"That's right, I remember vividly the month after you got kets, you got laid off for the first time... But you had a renter already lined up right?"*

(Dylan): I mean, I also had extra savings, but having that income lined up already, it was awesome! You get kinda used to getting laid off in Alberta these days. But with the income from my roommate, I can totally cover my bills and if I'm off for a couple months, it saves me from having to dip huge into my savings.

(Justin): *"So the House Hack has been a good strategy for you?"*

(Dylan): Absolutely!

(Justin): *"And you've told me as well, that you've taken a few trips recently and they've basically been paid for by your roommate income. It's like every six months you're texting me about a trip you've gone on. Where had you gone to recently?"*

(Dylan): The last three years, I've gone to England and Scotland for my birthday. Didn't go this year (2016), but every other year I've travelled to Belize for Christmas and Guatemala for a couple weeks. Basically a 1-2 week vacation in summer and a 1-2 week vacation in the winter.

(Justin): *"So what you're saying is 'Don't buy your own place because home ownership is a bad idea??"*

(Dylan): Yeah. Pretty much! hahaha…

Dylan's House Hack Summary:

Property Type:
2 BR / 2 BA townhouse w/ attached double garage, "Dual-Master" setup

Purchase Price:
Approx. $297,000

Extra $ Made From #HouseHack:
$47,000+/- over approx. 57 months, renting out second master suite @ $900/month, @ 10%+/- vacancy

---

DYLAN'S 2013 TESTIMONIAL

I met Justin on a Wednesday night at a cigar shop about five or six years ago.

About a year and a half or two years ago, I decided to buy my own place and asked Justin what I needed to do to save up and get prepared, get pre-approved.

Justin referred my to a great mortgage broker and we sat down, figured out the numbers and how much of a downpayment I'd need.

Fast forward to earlier this year, we went over some of the things I was aiming for in a home. The first night, Justin took me through over 10 or 12 places and from there, began to narrow things down to what I was really looking for.

Second time out, about a week later, we went to six or seven other properties and I decided that the home I'm in now is the one that was best suited to what I was after.

On a scale of 1 to 10, I'd give my place almost a 10 because as a new build, the front yard isn't quite done yet!

With my parents, the last place they bought, their agent didn't put a lot of time and effort into things. He was overly busy. Didn't want to put any effort into the process.

I've had a few friends complain about the same thing with their agents. Very strict hours. Just wants to get a sale done and move on. Or very high pressure.

Justin was different. He made a big effort to do

things to make it easier for my schedule, because I work until later in the day. Everybody I talk to, they say that Justin puts a lot more effort into every part of what he's doing for you.

The professionals he referred me to (mortgage broker, lawyer) were very accommodating. It was a really good experience dealing with them all - I'd recommend them 100%...And I've already recommended Justin to many friends and family, including my parents!

The whole reason I was thinking about buying a home with some rental potential is because somebody else is essentially buying your house and paying your interest for you. In my case, it's like I'm getting my house for half price...And I really like that idea!

And the other reason I was glad that I did what I did, after moving in and spending all this money on a downpayment, utility hook ups and deposits, moving costs...

...A month after this all happens, I got laid off.

I got a new job (I'm in the trades) about a couple weeks later, but because Justin helped me with marketing the second master suite that I'm renting out, and I had a tenant lined up, I was able to go through that period like it was nothing.

If you have some form of income coming in from your real estate, it can save you from the shock of losing your job all of a sudden.

The reason I picked this layout (new townhouse with two master suites) instead of a three bedroom with a second bedroom and an office, is exactly because of this!

Right now my mortgage payment works out to $100 more per month than the last house I was renting. So why would I pay rent, and pay somebody else's mortgage, when I can have my own house, have someone else pay ME rent, and in the end you're not just handing your money over to somebody else?

My tenant is paying 125$ more than one of my bi-weekly mortgage payments. So they're basically paying half my mortgage payments every year - 52 weeks in a year, 26 payments, he takes care of 13 of them!

You know the best part about having a great real estate agent who helped me make a smart choice? Got a renter that makes this a lot easier

ACTUAL MESSAGES FROM DYLAN: (@R: 2013, @L: 2015)

You make my day with your updates re renters etc! So glad you're WINNING in spite of the negatives in the economy ow.

Delive

Just had a girl come to look at my spare room. She said she was looking to save some money and buy a place in 6 months or so. I told her about what a great real estate dude you were while she was here

Love ya!! Tell her about our home buying seminar. Next one is Monday night.

"SHARP SINGLE WOMAN USES HER #HOUSEHACK INCOME TO PAY FOR OUT-OF-POCKET MEDICAL COSTS LIKE A BOSS!"

Sandy is a trooper. A warrior. The girl doesn't give up. Not only did I have the privilege of calling her a client, she's since entered the real estate industry and has now become a trusted business partner at EMPOWER Real Estate Group.

There's a good chance you'll meet here if you schedule a Consultation at EMPOWER HQ. And if you have the pleasure of being represented by her during YOUR home-searching process, trust me when I say that her "Never Stay Down" attitude will serve you well. Here's her #HouseHack story…

(Justin): *"How did we meet?"*

(Sandy): My friend and personal trainer referred me to Justin to help me find my own place. After getting out of a previous relationship where both my partner and I had owned two homes together, when we parted ways I ended up renting and wanted to get back on the owning-side of the real estate fence.

(Justin): *"Where you always thinking about potentially renting to a roommate?"*

(Sandy): Originally I had a different line of thinking about purchasing a home. I want to do it independently. (Because I'm a woman, hear me roar!).

(Justin): *"What changed your perspective?"*

(Sandy): Perspective on goals and where I wanted to be in 3, 5, 10 years. I realized that I was exerting more energy than I needed to, trying to pay all my bills on my own. That's why I got a place where I could get a roommate/renter, so I could expedite the goals I wanted to accomplish.

(Justin): *"What were some of those goals?"*

(Sandy): Saving for retirement. But mostly I wanted to travel. (For instance, Panama-I had already been to, but wanted to go to: Mexico, Galápagos Islands, and Peru). Peru-2015, Galápagos-2013, Mexico-2014, Panama-2010/11). The money I've taken in over the few years I've owned my property, obviously it hasn't been fully occupied the entire time, nor did the income pay entirely for these goals. But they certainly helped me out financially in being able to accomplish paying for portions of my travels! Every few thousand dollars helps right?

(Justin): *"Would you say that over the last few years of owning your property, that the income from your roommates contributed (at all) to you accomplishing those goals?"*

(Sandy): Absolutely! Also, I don't know if it's pertinent, a lot of the income that came from roommates also went to paying for the costs of rehab (chiropractor, personal trainer, acupressure, massage) after I discovered I had issues with my back/spine/hip. A lot of those costs were covered, but I had tapped out my coverage and if I wanted to continue progressing with my back rehabilitation, I needed to pay out of pocket. Having the additional income certainly helped me out quite a bit.

(Justin): *"Let's talk about what type of property you ended up getting…"*

(Sandy): As you know (because you were my agent!) it's a carriage-home style townhouse. It's got a double attached garage. And I've got two bedrooms and one bathroom.

(Justin): *"So you rent out one bedroom?"*

(Sandy): Yup! I don't at the present time, but I did off and on for the past three years.

(Justin): *"How much were you charging?"*

(Sandy): My wonderful roommates had the privilege of paying $650-$700/per month whereas renting my place out by itself, they'd easily be paying over double that in this market.

(Justin): *"What are some of the challenges of renting to a roommate and what would you do differently, or advise people to consider, if they're going to do their own "House Hack"?"*

(Sandy): One thing would be having a complete understanding of household duties: who's responsible for what and when (who cleans the bathroom, when). I had a friend living with me one time who was into martial arts, and she had the habit of washing her ninja-attire every day to be clean for the next class. We agreed she'd pay a bit extra for utilities as other roommates didn't use the laundry as often/much.

(Justin): *"Overall, would you say your #HouseHack experience was negative or positive?"*

(Sandy): Obviously positive. There have been a couple obvious benefits. It's catapulted me to being able to achieve other goals that would've taken longer to accomplish without having the extra income. When you take on living with someone else, obviously it changes some aspects of your freedom to live/do what you please in your own home. But overall, I'll also just say that before jumping into a #HouseHack, you need to understand what you enjoy doing. Are you always going to be home or not? Bringing people over or not? Is your roommate going to be doing the same thing? I'd encourage people to ensure that the individual(s) they select to have as renters/roommates have lifestyles and habits that are conducive to your own enjoyment of the home and your lifestyle.

(Justin): *"Excellent advice! Thanks for sharing your story Sandy!"*

Sandy's House Hack Summary:

Property Type:
2 BR / 1 BA townhouse w/ garage

Purchase Price:
Approx. $220,000

Extra $ Made From #HouseHack:
$7,000 - $8,000 +/- over approx. 36 months, renting out second bedroom intermittently @ $650-$700/month

---

This Next One Is A Good One...

If You're Local, Whyte Ave Area
is a Terrific Spot for
#HouseHacking!

:-)

"LOCAL REAL ESTATE ENTREPRENEUR & WIFE OFFSET REDUCED INCOME DURING MATERNITY LEAVE WITH BASEMENT SUITE INCOME!"

The writing of this chapter will be a bit of a departure from the rest of this volume, as it'd be strange to have an interview or conversation about my experiences, with myself.

Lol.

So instead, I'll just write my thoughts and responses to some of the handful of questions I've been asking the other individuals in this book…

(Justin, ie. Me): *"When did you #HouseHack? Do you still currently #HouseHack?"*

(Me, also...):   In the summer of 2009, my wife Kate became pregnant with our first daughter. At the time, we were living in a loft on Jasper Ave that we had purchased just shortly before getting married a couple years prior. (Lesson #1: Don't buy a 1 Bedroom loft if having kids anytime in the near future is a possibility!).

Our plans of getting into a larger home became an immediate priority, so the house hunting started. Because we had met, and (back then) still spent a lot of our time in the popular Whyte Ave/Old Strathcona area of Edmonton, we felt it would be a great area to find a home to start raising our family.

In the fall of 2009, just a couple weeks before Kate's birthday, we closed on a great bungalow in the neighbourhood of Hazeldean.

(An interesting side note: Two years earlier, after we had come back from our honeymoon, I had written down a few goals for the coming years. One of which was to be living in a house off Whyte avenue, with a basement suite to supplement income and cover some expenses, and that we'd also be in the midst of starting our family, growing my real estate business, and that we'd accomplish this from our new home base and be moving in prior to Kate's birthday at the end of October. I NEVER saw that piece of paper again for nearly two years, until we moved into our new home...

About two weeks after moving in, while unpacking a random box, I picked up a book to place on our book shelf and out slipped this piece of paper where I'd written these goals down. And there, staring me in the face, was the written goal we were now living, and had accomplished essentially to the very month, as predicted! **You WILL find what you're looking for if you are motivated and have faith...**_**Even when you forgot that you set the intention**_**!**)

(Q): *"What Type of Home were you searching for?"*

(J): Being in real estate, and having investor clients, and also reading about real estate investing over the years, it only made sense to consider owning a property that generated some income just for living in it and renting extra space out to a tenant. In our case, we were specifically looking for a home with a secondary suite. This was especially important for us as, expecting our first child, we didn't want to have an actual room mate and share living spaces (kitchen, bathroom, etc). We wanted an entirely separate dwelling, which meant a separate basement suite was a must.

(Q): *"And why was it important to you to implement the #HouseHack strategy?"*

(J):   Kate was going on maternity leave, so our household income was going to take a drop for a bit. But even if that wasn't the case, it's not like we absolutely needed an entire house to ourselves for just one couple with one baby. I figured, if we were going to own a property but there was potential for the property to put some income in our pocket every month to offset the costs of ownership, that'd be a huge plus and wouldn't require much of an adjustment in terms of budget, or the type of home we needed.

(Q): *"How much money were you taking in while you owned the home, and how long did you own it for?"*

(J): We closed on the home in October 2009. I spent a few months, during evenings and weekends, doing some renovations to the basement suite to update it a bit (mostly the downstairs bathroom). Our first tenant moved in around March 2010 and was with us for three years. They paid $645/month. After that, we had two different tenants. One stayed less than half a year. The next tenant signed on and was actually still renting, and was assumed by the buyer who purchased our home, when we sold it in early 2014. Each of those tenants paid $675/month. In the four and a half years (approximate) that we owned the home, and not counting the few months after we purchased where I was doing work on the basement suite, we literally had less than three months vacancy: Only a week or two between our first long-term tenant, and the next tenant. And then not even two months between the next tenant and our last tenant. Over the course of that time, we took in roughly $29,000 in rental income. (And it's important to note, we claimed every penny of it on our tax returns and paid income tax on the rent we received, even when we received payment in cash).

(Q): *"Was it easy to get tenants?"*

(J): Granted, I've got a bit of an advantage being in the real estate profession, so marketing for potential tenants wasn't that difficult a challenge for me. In fact, many other clients who have also done the #HouseHack strategy, or have outright purchased separate rental properties, I've lent a hand in terms of tenant marketing strategies. But the biggest factor that simplified the process for us was purchasing a home in an area where rental demand was quite high. Being off Whyte Ave, there's always an abundance of people looking to rent in the area because of it's convenience and proximity to basically the entire city. Hazeldean, and the entire Whyte Ave corridor from University of Alberta east towards the Bonnie Doon area, is essentially smack in the geographic middle of the city of Edmonton.

(Q): *"Did that mean you rented to students because you were near a University? Did you have to put up with partying and irresponsible 'young' tenants?"*

(J): No, not at all. In fact, while we had a few applications from students on the rare times we had to advertise to fill a vacancy, we didn't rent to a single student the entire time we owned the property. Our first tenant had a steady job in the west end of town, but she wanted to be close to her friends in Sherwood park and have quick access to shopping and amenities. Our other two tenants had jobs in the Southside and worked full time.

(Q): *"What were some of the challenges with executing the #HouseHack strategy?"*

(J): Early on during our first tenant experience, I had a bit of a scare. (The tenant is still friends with my wife and I to this day, and we look back and laugh at it now!)

This tenant, she had a friend help her move in, and the fellow drove his pickup truck into our back yard which wasn't fenced at the time. They were moving in her mattress and box spring, and this old house had very tight corners going to the basement. So it was about 10pm at night, my wife is in the bedroom with our new born, and she wakes me up asking "What's all the noise coming from the back door??" I bolted out of bed and quietly tiptoed to the rear entrance expecting to encounter a burglar. When I went downstairs, I was literally ready to jump on whoever I saw and start the process of forcibly removing them from the house....And then I saw our tenant, wide eyed and worried, and her stunned friend looking at me, wondering if he was about to get a beat down!

Once things settled down, I politely asked them to perhaps consider moving any belongings in during daylight hours so as not to wake us, or have any confusion of identity as to who was downstairs. So, part of that was the tenant not considering someone was living upstairs above her suite. An honest mistake for someone who's never rented a place all to herself. But mostly it was my fault for not setting expectations about moving in, and appropriate times for such activity. I learned that lesson, and had to revisit it once with our second tenant when she had a couple friends over and was being a bit too loud too late in the evening. I only had to text her from upstairs once, asking her to respect that it was late in the evening (11pm) and we could hear her immediately ask her friends to "keep it down" and it was never an issue after that. Our third tenant, we barely ever knew she was home or away, except to see her coming and going from work or heading out with friends.

(Q): *"So was that a huge downside, having someone living downstairs?"*

(J): A lot of it had to do with owning an older home. Sound proofing between the floors was almost nonexistent. But it comes down to setting expectations with those living with you, and also respecting that they have a right to the use and enjoyment of their own living space. Much of the friction can be eliminated entirely before it occurs though by making sure you do a good job of screening your potential tenant/ roommate, trusting your gut, and only allowing someone to live in your property that will absolutely get along with you and your lifestyle.

Also, we were very up front with all potential applicants about the fact that we had young children upstairs and they'd need to be ok with the fact that the kids would do what kids do: cry, play with toys, sometimes be up at odd hours of the night, etc. We were fortunate that all three tenants were very respectful, mature (despite being all in their early or mid 20's when they signed their rental agreements), and had an understanding that we were upstairs with young children. Just goes to show that it's really up to the owner of the property to select and pick the right people that are the right fit.

(Q): *"What would you do differently?"*

(J): Looking back, we were fortunate to have the insights we did about the rental demand in the areas we were searching for a home. But the biggest failing we had was 100% my fault and zero fault of my Saint-of-a-wife, Kate. And that was being so focused on finding a place with a rental suite that we didn't account for future family expansion (ie. Having more kids).

You'd think "we" (ie. *I*) would have learned with our first place: A 1 bedroom loft on Jasper Ave. The home we bought in Hazeldean was a four bedroom home, which included a 1 bedroom self-contained basement suite. But there was only two bedrooms on the main level, which meant that the third bedroom (which served double-duty as my home office, and as a guest bedroom when family or friends were in from out of town), was in the basement off on its own.

When we had our first daughter, this was no problem. Kate and I had the master bedroom to ourselves, and our newborn had the smaller bedroom as the nursery. But when we had our second daughter a year and a half later, we made the decision to switch rooms. Which meant "mom and dad" got the smaller bedroom with the tiny closet (horrible, because as Kate will tell you, I have too many shirts), and our newborn and then-toddler both shared the larger master bedroom because it was the only room that could accommodate both the crib and the toddler bed. We weren't about to put a baby or toddler in a room by themselves on another floor, nor were we about to put ourselves downstairs and our kids upstairs all by themselves.

So that was a very shortsighted error on my part. In retrospect, it would've been wiser to make sure we had THREE bedrooms on the main level, regardless of what was in the basement. But I know this now, and I get a good laugh from young newlyweds and couples starting families who come to the brokerage for a consultation and are in similar situation to where Kate and I were years ago. For most, it would seem this is common sense, but common sense isn't all that common when you're wrapped up in the emotion of buying your first home, or starting a family together. I've had more than one grateful set of buyers thank me for pointing this out before they made the same mistake!

(Q): *"Overall would you say your house-hack experience was a positive one?"*

(J): Absolutely. Definitely not without it's drawbacks. I don't claim to whitewash the potential downsides. You've got to know what you're getting into, whether you've got a place with a separate suite or you're doing the rent-a-spare-room strategy. But overall, Kate and I are glad to have benefited from the additional income over the years we owned the property. It helped us a lot given her income went down significantly while on maternity leave for two pregnancies.

Justin & Kate's House Hack Summary:

Property Type:
4 BR / 2 BA 1950's Bungalow w/ garage; 2 BR / 1 BA up + 1 BR down, 1 BR / 1 BA Suite down

Purchase Price:
Approx. $310,000

Extra $ Made From #HouseHack:
$29,000 +/- over approx. 45 months, renting out basement suite near Whyte Ave / 99 Street.

"SAVVY POLITICAL CONSULTANT SCORES SWEET PAD FOR HIS FIRST HOME...ALONG WITH A WIN-WIN SETUP RENTING TO A GOOD FRIEND"

Dan's story is similar to Dylan in story (pg. 57) in that, after many months of searching for the right home, evaluating lifestyle and needs, Dan ended up choosing a home with a "Dual Master" setup (ie. TWO "Master Bedrooms", large rooms with attached and private ensuite bathrooms), the latter of which he rents to a good friend of his.

While sitting through the home inspection on the property he now owns, Dan and I did this interview about his thoughts on #HouseHack, life, finances, and a bit of politics for good measure! Here's the summary of that interview...

(Justin): *"So Dan, can you tell the readers how we met?"*

(Dan): We met when we attended school together. But after we graduated, it was a while before we reconnected. I reached out to (you) on Facebook. I knew you were in the real estate industry. Probably almost three years ago. Said I'm in the market looking to make some decisions surrounding real estate, and you had me come by the office for a chat. I hummed and hawed for several months, then I gave you a call after I (then) figured out that I wanted a gorgeous, attractive, trendy bachelor pad condo downtown.

(Justin): *"What made you reach out to me VS other agents you know? What struck you to 'Call Justin'?"*

(Dan): For the work that I do in government, it's fair to say I'm very well-connected and know a lot of people. In terms of macro thinking, I didn't want to go to my dad and just ask for an agent from his Rolodex. I wanted to do my own thing. I didn't want to talk to somebody who might pick up the phone and say "Hey, your kid was in my office". I wanted this to be an independent process without dad-connections involved.

In terms of reaching out to you (vs other agents that I know); three things struck me:

1) First was having you on social media. Seeing the "EMPOWER" thing, it was never just "I'm a realtor, I sell houses", but you genuinely cared about the people

you helped, you were active and updated your social media regularly, the fact you had this brand-thing going on that stood for more than just "selling a house" to somebody, I mean, it could've gone cheesy (like, 'Justin thinks he's Tony Robbins") but instead I really felt like you took the time to understand me and what my goals were, you understand the market very well, and it was clear you took pride in what you're doing.

2). Because there's a history (we grew up together), granted a lot of years had gone by since we went to school together, but I felt that because there's a past history, you weren't going to be someone who's just going to bullshit me.

And then 3) My long-term thinking is, this will be the first step in a longer, multiple-property journey... And I want whoever I connected with on this first deal to be my "Go-To" pro for the future. That I could build a good working relationship with and help me achieve those long-term goals.

(Justin): *"You mentioned social media. Why did that make a difference for you?"*

(Dan): Your social media presence made the difference for me. Being in the comms game in politics, looking at your social media, it was well thought out. It wasn't sh*t. That was a big thing for me. You "get it".

(Justin): *"You talk about long-term goals of owning more property, in light of that, where do you see this property fitting into those goals? And why is that* *important to you overall?"*

(Dan):   I want to be financially independent.   And that's not to say I don't want to work.   I'm always going to be working hard to make a difference in whatever cause I take on.   But, for me, it means "having assets and resources that work hard for me, so I can be selective about the opportunities I pursue".

What I mean is, if I'm financially independent, I can perhaps take on an opportunity that may not be as financially rewarding as other options, but has the potential to   have bigger payoff in terms of my interests and values and making a difference in the community.   Service-type stuff.   So I don't want to be held hostage by employers, salaries, just to make my bills each month.   I'd rather take hold of the situation on my own. Gives me more control.

So in terms of my thinking, long-term strategy for me is, there's ups and downs and swings in the economy, but in terms of our process, the more I think about it, if I can weather the valleys, we can climb to exceptional heights.

Real estate is, I mean, people have been getting rich off of it for forever. (If!) You do it right, you do it smart.   And my thing is I don't see myself as the next Donald Trump with my name on everything…I'd like to have a nice little portfolio of assets, get like a small density apartment building, build up some assets that create income and allow me to focus on time and energy on making a difference.

That's the long term vision. And ultimately, land in a

place that I want to be "DSP Headquarters". And that's maybe 10-15-20 yrs down the road. I'm looking long-term.

(Justin): *"With what you're focusing on doing with this place, let's walk through what you were originally looking for and how we ended up here..."*

(Dan): Here's the thing, and this is life-advice not just real estate advice. Today, it's 2017. You've got more computing power in your hand with that phone than the astronauts who went to the moon. Information has been so democratized, unlike anything that anybody could have ever anticipated even 20 years ago. So your access to, now, frame it in the real estate perspective: You've got a million realtors, you've got a bunch of different brokerages, you've got fly-by-nights and big corporate franchises, you've got Comfree and DIY on kijiji, there's a PILE of options.

It's like WebMD: "I have a rash at the end of my finger..." so I hop online and plug in "I have a rash at the end of my finger" on google, so you plug that into your phone, and webMD gives you a thousands answers, ranging from "Your finger is about to fall off!" To "You have a staph infection from an ingrown hair in your cuticle..." so then you get frantic and overwhelmed.

And this is the point: You're overwhelmed with massive amounts of information and (mostly) unqualified opinions. Is it this or is it that? Is this doctor legit? It's the same thing across all professions now, that people think that they know more than they do because they have access to all this information.

So...with all of that being said, from my perspective, there are a lot of good ideas. But it doesn't necessarily make that the RIGHT idea for me. And that's where we started.

My initial thinking was "Bachelor Pad Downtown". I go to Credo for coffee. I wanted that Metro urban lifestyle. I start looking at stuff and shootin' it off to you. I remember we went to that 8th floor unit at a building on Jasper Ave. It looked cool. A lot of space. Exposed ceiling. Great unit. I was wondering "Why is it so cheap?" And then we get there and you're telling me "We'll, the condo fees are, whatever they were, $675/month, and there's no titled parking stall I've got to rent a parking stall, in fact there's no parking at all, there's barely a reserve fund, and a special assessment is coming" so THAT was an eye opener for me.

Intellectually, you know "Yes, condos have condo fees". But until you get into a place you've been thinking about and looking at on a screen, and then really evaluating at a visceral level, in-person, if that's the right option for you...That's something else. And you helped me do that.

We went from bachelor pads and condos, to townhouses with grass out front and a bit of fence, then eventually to houses. But I was worried about "Should I get a house? Can I afford a house? Do I get an older house? What if it needs fixing?" And all that stuff.

We went through all of these options, and it was like

a two-year process, and as we went and looked at all of these things, it started to clarify for me what really are my priorities. Really, my priorities are, there's only thee: the first is to live in a place I am comfortable in. What that mean is I don't want to live in a fixer-upper. For me, I want to be comfortable where I am, and that needed to be factored in to my decision. I could've gotten a place that was a lot cheaper, but six months in, I'd be coming home and wanting to sell the place because even though I was saving money, I'd be hating where I lived.

For me, it was also being aware of what my lifestyle is and what I could be comfortable. But not so custom/comfortable for ME that it wasn't re-saleable in between. So was this place "my house"? Or was it straight up "investment"? Or was it a bridge between the two?

And you did a great job at our first meeting at your brokerage, where you told me I need to be clear on what this is and isn't going to be. Ultimately, what's important to me. You talked about CLARITY. And I thought initially I could do "Just an investment" and not worry about being comfortable. And we looked at a few places that fit that bill. And they probably would've been great investment properties down the road. But after getting clarity on my priorities, I thought: "Not going to happen!".

We looked at a couple things as well, that was more like my dream castle, my bachelor space, my home base for the next decade, right? But it was on the higher end of my budget and that didn't really work for me either.

So comfort, what really is my goal long term, and then the third piece of it for me was the affordability part. I know what my lifestyle is. I know I kind of wanted a bridge, a place that was a good investment but that I could also be comfortable in for the next 3-5 years. But, once you've checked those boxes, I don't have $600k to spend on a "house on the golf course".

I don't want to cheap out on something that was 50 years old and needed a roof next year. So: 1) Short, Medium, and Long-Term goals, 2) Comfortability, and 3) Affordability.

Aside from that, I had ancillary things happen that I had not anticipated that also changed my thinking on that. What happened to me is exactly what you just said in terms of roommate situations. A friend of mine and I go out to have drinks and dinner and she says "Dan, am I ever tired of paying $1400-$1500 bucks a month rent, a condo with elevators and nine trips for groceries and I have a dog and I want a yard..." and I'm like "Yeah, I'm kind of over paying all this money too, it'd be nice to kind of mitigate some of these expenses..."

Then the conversation continues to: "I don't want a room mate though" and she says "I don't have to have a room mate either, there's only a handful of people I"d ever consider living with..." and I'm like "Yeah, me too. You'd probably be on my list though." and she says "Yeah, you'd be on my list too..."

PAUSE

We're both like, "Oh, wait a minute... Are we talking

about this now? Maybe this makes a certain amount of sense..." And so that altered my thinking. It was sort of a half-hearted conversation in passing that then got really serious when the topic of our respective leases came up.

We both had about two months each left on our own rentals. So that changed my thinking all of a sudden to, which was now "I'm going to live with somebody" how do we make that work? How do we make sure we have enough space to not want encroach on each other, but it still be manageable, that I can still afford the place if he/she moves out, I still need to be able to make my bills, and even if/when I may not have another roommate.

So that shifted the thinking. And out of that came an important criteria which is, I come back to Justin and say "Justin, I'm thinking house/townhouse now, let's ditch the condos but heres the deal: I need TWO master bedrooms. None of this master-bedroom-and-two-little-little-other-two-bedrooms type-places. Let's find something that has two master bedroom suites, which eliminated a lot of things, but it shook out some key stuff. So that accelerated the process because there was a handful of things to look at now instead of fifty.

(Justin): *"On the topic of townhouse/house VS half-duplex, the price point, total cost of ownership is an important concept. I mean, you can pay a lot less for an apartment condo, but that downtown loft unit, I took two sets of clients through it when it was vacant because it stayed on the market so long...But it was*

'Super Cheap' at $230k, but the condo fees were over $600/month, you could've bought a $400k house when you look at the 'Total Cost of Ownership'...So what was your entire thought process around that and what did you say to yourself to stay on budget?"

Dan: I don't think, I had ever really sat down and looked at what a $300 or $400 condo fee would translate into in terms of total financed mortgage amount until you mentioned it. I sent you a note, "Found some townhouses, can we go?" These were the Brookfield units. We talked about it. You said they were a great builder. Good units. Nice area. Would've been great. But the condo fee is about $160/month.

And then it's "Well, it's $160, but you have to look at rising costs long-term with condo fees, because it's up to the board, not just me, to decide "ok, now we're going to pay $250 instead of $160" which is totally the reality for a lot of these newer places in the first year or two after purchasing," you had told me.

Also, the concept of "I've bought something but I don't control the entire structure of what I own" piece is in there as well. That was a good lesson in perspectives: All-in, out the door, the thing was $290k, 1200 sqft, two master bedrooms, really nice and brand new, fully upgraded. That looked attractive. Mortgage payment was $1250 with the down payment I had anticipated...But then you add the condo fee. So, being very conservative, let's assume $250 not the $160 it is now, so a $250 condo fee equates to now about a $320k purchase price when you consider the condo fee is equivalent to that additional bump in price for a non-condominium home with no condo fee.

In terms of going from the townhouse and saying ok there's a detached home, Single Family Dwelling, in this area I like, and it's "here" and the economy is "here" these are the ancillary pieces now, right? The room mate situation changes things. Economy isn't the greatest at the moment. Confidence in the market is low. Interest rates are low. People need out from things perhaps they were too Bullish on, and that's a mistake I have to be cognizant of not making myself.

And so the big question with this (detached home VS townhouse), and concerns about Trudeau's "stress test" and mortgage qualifying, I hummed and hawed about that for a bit, and I finally said "Well, I can hum and haw, or I can finally call a mortgage broker, let's do this, lets figure it out!"

So when it came down to it, I could qualify for what I needed, the numbers worked, and i'm certainly at the top end of what my comfort level was, I'm going to have to shift my priorities and lifestyle a bit to accommodate, have a couple less Old Fashions and a couple less Cuban cigars every month, but I'm at the top of my comfort level, I qualify for far more, but I have a limit that I'd like to stay within, but I got a screaming deal because of those ancillary factors, I have some security with additional income from a room mate that's committing for a period of time, I have no condo corporation telling me what I can or can't do at my property, or who can just walk in and up the fees on me.

And at the end of the day, something that you said really resonated with me, and that was "Owning the dirt is always a solid long-term investment". I think you were quoting John Jacob Astor.

So I checked all of my boxes. I got the dual masters in this house. Long term, that may limit me 10 yrs from now when I actually sell the house, but for my lifestyle for the next 3-5 years, it's perfect. And for holding onto the house when I shift to renting the entire property out when I move on, in a roommate scenario, the future tenants have a lot of benefit from the setup. If in ten years I decide to sell it, I'm going to benefit from the growth of my equity even if I sell for the same price. Or maybe I keep it forever and just rent it out.

The point is, I feel like, now, I have far more options than I did before looking at one bedroom bachelor pad condos. I have a wider market to sell to, or rent to. I don't have to factor a condo fee in now, when I'm renting the place. That $250 goes into my jeans instead of needing to be paid for. Of all the things I did, I'm a smart guy, I think I'm reasonably savvy, but I'm not an expert at real estate. So being savvy, I called somebody who IS an expert to help me.

I had sat down and written on paper, "Options A… B… C… D…", written out the pros and cons, looked at the costs, etc. and once I did that...

(Justin): *"HOLD ON…You ACTUALLY put pen-to-paper and analyzed a few things?? WOW…What a concept…"*

(Ed: Said with dripping sarcasm as we require all potential clients to fill out a Pre-Consultation questionnaire before coming to meet us).

(Dan): Yeah, I know. right? Which I guarantee a lot of people DON'T do that...

(Justin): *"NO. They don't..."*

(Dan): ...But having, and I'm very visual, having all four of them, in front of me, all right there, the thing that pushed me to the top end of my comfort level financially was the thing that made the most sense for short term, medium term, and long term.

(Justin): *"Let's talk for a second about your friend/ roommate/tenant for a moment if we could. What's she paying you and what does that include?"*

(Ed: At this point, Dan was in the process of finalizing his purchase during this interview so the figures below are his projections. As of publication, his renter had stayed, for $1000/month, for about a year +/-)

(Dan): Basically what we discussed, and we haven't totally landed 100% on numbers, but what we both seem to be comfortable with is $1000/month. If this were a master with two small bedrooms, sharing one common bathroom, it probably wouldn't be feasible to expect that much. The thing is, this dual master setup we have, she has a private space for herself and that kind of made sense to her. The other piece is, given that we were friends, I knew that this amount was in line with the going rate for other similar rental options (smaller one bedroom apartments) in the area, but more importantly, that it was giving her a chance to save thousands a year on living costs because she was renting and paying for this other condo all by herself.

She gets a fenced back yard for her dog. She gets a garage space for her car. There's TONS of value.

(Justin): *"It's literally like she's paying $1000/ month to rent your entire house, but she shares all but about 300 sq ft of it with you, basically..."*

(Dan): That's right. That's the thing. She was paying nearly $1500/month before for a one bedroom condo down the Henday in the southside. Nice size place. But wow.... Why NOT put $5000/year in your pocket?? And she gets the comfort of living in a house VS having a hundred neighbours in a busy condo complex. Now, I end up getting a great roommate, and I get to take her dog to the off-leash park, but I don't have to worry about any of the vet bills... hahaha.

But in all seriousness, it's a great arrangement for us both. So much value to both of us. And for me, it's like I literally found $1000/month extra free money, in the sense that I need it to NOT factor into what I could afford. That's the fundamental thing. Free money to me: Someone is using 300 sqft of my house, is out half the time, but we hang out once in a while. All of my hard costs, are mine. I can afford them.

And THEN because I got a friend who's fun to hang out with, living in my house now, I get $12,000 a year...

(Justin): *"Which is how much over the course of a five year mortgage term??"*

(Dan): Well, if she hangs with me for five years, that's $60,000...

(Justin): *"Oh, but what if she only sticks around for 12 months???"*

(Dan): Well that's the other thing, right? It's still $12,000 I wouldn't otherwise have had. Or say $36,000 if its three years.

(Justin): *"Sounds like the start of a nice downpayment on Property Number Two..."*

(Dan): EXACTLY.

(Justin): *"If your present circumstance with a roommate already being lined up, had that not occurred, where would you look to find a potential roommate/renter?"*

(Dan): That's an interesting question... Had this not just fallen into my lap, I don't know if I would have come up with a plan to have a roommate. I'm just that comfortable on my own. Now that being said...if I got it into my head that I was going to do a roommate scenario, I'd have started with my closest circle of friends that I know are renting elsewhere or interested in moving out maybe for the first time (early to mid-20's, etc). I'd have pitched them on how they could save money, or move out for the first time and pay a lot less than if they did it on their own. I would've gone through my FaceBook friend's list, or look at people I've spent a lot of time with, people that I already have a sense of their habits. Maybe we've spent two weeks in Mexico together on a trip, or something like that, you know? My preference would be somebody I already know and have some pre-existing relationship with.

(Justin): *"What are some of your goals with the money you'll be receiving from your roommate?"*

(Dan): I'd like a Porsche naturally,... lol. But seriously, I think for me, it becomes (the $40k I squirrel away or whatever), becomes the basis of an investment portfolio with a money manager. Or I may also have it set aside for when I'm ready to buy the next place. Ideally, in the next decade or so, I'd like to have a few places. Maybe five places. But I'm not going to cry if I have only three by then....The thing is, and I'll say this too, one of the other considerations I have is, in addition to building that equity, if I'm buying money at 2.5% over the next few years, and I'm getting 5.5, 6.5, 7.5% ROI on money I have socked elsewhere...why would I pull cash out of an 8% return when I can buy cash at 2.5%??

(Justin): *"Makes sense! Thanks so much for your time, Dan!"*

(Dan): No problem! Can't wait for the next one!

Dan's House Hack Projections:

Property Type:
Newer 2 BR / 2 BA, Two Storey w/ double garage, "Dual-Master" setup

Purchase Price:
Approx. $360,000

PROJECTED $$ For #HouseHack:
$12,000 +/- over approx. 12 months, at $1000/month including utilities, and parking spot in double garage…

Nearly $60,000 over first 5-year mortgage term if second master-suite is rented the entire time…

If You Don't Want Room Mates
And Straight Up Want Rental
Property…

…G.Yeezy's Story Is What's Up!

"G.YEEZY GOES FROM DROPPING $3K/MONTH MAINTAINING ONE $750K PROPERTY PERSONALLY... TO OWNING JUST UNDER* $1-MILLION IN REAL ESTATE AND #HOUSEHACKING OWNERSHIP COSTS DOWN TO ONLY $500/MONTH!"

So "G.Yeezy" is NOT this client's real name. For privacy reasons, she's opted to use a pseudonym to relay his story and experiences regarding the #HouseHack Strategy. Part of this is because, due to successfully implementing this strategy and taking it to the next level, he's built an impressive portfolio of even more properties than what we'll discuss below. I don't blame her. ("Wait a sec, you said "him" two sentences ago, and "her" just a second ago. Which one is it?...". For me to know, and you to guess. *wink*).

Rest assured though, G.Yeezy is a real-life individual who has done a really good job at implementing his own #HouseHack and leveraging it into a portfolio that now, if he or she were to entirely quit their regular 9-5, would basically make them financially independent (ie. Basic living expenses covered by after-tax income received from cashflow from investments acquired, in this case, in real estate).

And while G.Yeezy is a long-time client, it wasn't only a few short years ago that she took on this journey and went from owning one property, and paying for it 100% with his own income...To now, controlling a modest but sizeable portfolio in the low-$7-figure+ range with gross annual cashflow exceeding the low-$6-figure+ mark. After paying related mortgage payments, property taxes, insurance, maintenance costs, accounting for income tax, and saving for future reinvestment, G.Yeezy is a shining example of how the #HouseHack can pyramid you very effectively and simply into a position of financial independence inside a short time-frame if one is motivated and maximizes the resources available to them. (Side note: She also did start off with a property that had a large amount of equity. However, don't let his prior circumstances dissuade you from the power of the #HouseHack. You can do it to, once you recognize the power of Compounding small wins over a longer period of time!).

G.Yeezy stopped by a recent EMPOWER Christmas

Party and took some time to answer a few questions, which are summarized and transcribed below...

(Justin): *"So in this book, we talk about the concept of #HouseHack, something you're very very familiar with. And that's taking a different approach to the spare space in your current residence, either a spare bedroom in a condo or townhouse, all the way to owning a property with a secondary suite in the basement. Or in your case, leveraging that into now multiple rental properties. And I think the common misconception is that to "invest" in real estate, one has to buy like 50 condos, or a 24 unit apartment complex. And for so many people, that's so far out of reach. And for many, even owning just a second house that's a rental property may seem like a bit of a stretch. But your beginnings were really interesting, because you went from having a big place just outside the city, and now we're selling it, and you think "Why buy a place when I can get a place and also have money coming in in the form of a suite?...And if I'm downsizing, and I got all this capital, why wouldn't I do that, and get a condo to live in and get a house with a suite and rent BOTH units out instead of living onsite?"*

And then that progressed to getting TWO places with suites, and living in one unit and renting the other three out. So I guess, for you, because you're very unique in this set of interviews for this book, in that you basically said "While I'm at it, let's not do ONE #HouseHack, let's do TWO and get TWO places and put basement suites in them...", what was the Big AHA moment for you, the thought process that took you from "Let's downsize" to "Let's get a condo and a rental property with two suites" to "Let's get TWO places and put suites in BOTH..."?

(G):   Sort of what I was telling Sandy earlier, I had done a number of years of time share rentals. Vacation property type stuff.   And with getting rid of the acreage, it was like "Hey, let's take it to the net level. IF I've been doing vacation property rentals for years, let's do REAL property rentals and try it with actual homes."

I had done a lot of "income property" watching, you know, the HGTV-style shows that you're so fond of *sarcasm* (*Ed: As a real estate agent, I have a love-hate relationship with HGTV shows...*).   But the premise of it was 'Why not use your money'.

I come from a financial-services industry, and there's no difference taking money and investing in some fund or stock and then cashing out and having capital appreciation. Whereas with rental real estate, it's just a different type of cashflow management.   You're looking at your mortgage, and also at which you can write off a number of your expenses because it's an investment property, and for me, it's all about deductions. So if you can deduct against your rental income, it's not a bad thing. Because the net effect is that you're not going to pay that much marginally more than if you had gains on capital appreciation of say an investment in equities. And you have a tangible asset at the end of the day. (Whereas stocks, you can't do much with them except buy or sell or maybe collect a dividend...But a house, you or someone else, can always live in it. It has REAL value.).

So that was kind of my thinking on why I wanted to get into the real estate space. And the other part of it, touching on your comments about downsizing, is that I just realized at the end of the day "Hey, what do I REALLY need for space?" (Referring to the large acreage G.Yeezy formerly owned). That's one of the things we were talking about. Yeah, it's nice to have that super big home, but then you've got all this space collecting dust, rooms that don't get used, etc. What are you comfortable with, re: useable space, and having some non-useable space being used by someone else, and having that space pay for things like your mortgage.

(Justin): *"Which makes perfect sense, why pay for your bills when you can have someone else willing sign up for the privilege of doing that FOR you, right?"*

(G): Yup!

(Justin): *"So, what was it like...We initially stated with "Get a house, put a suite in it" and then you evolved that to, the in between stage of "Get a house, put a suite in, and then get a condo to rent...", which turned into "Let's get two places at the same time, put basement suites in both, AT THE SAME TIME..."*

(G):   Well, we did look at some condos and I was thinking "Okay, I could do the condo thing..." and then buy a rental property, but we got talking about "What would rent easily?" And about "Location", which led me to really consider what the BEST use of my funds from the acreage sale was going to be. So if I'm going to buy a condo at $200k, ok...can I use that $200k, add another $150k onto that, and buy something that's going to be better.

Because the condo, if I'm living there, I can't write off anything of that, because it's a personal residence. NO deductions. Whereas if I can live up/down, in a place with a basement suite, and rent the extra suite out, that made much more sense. And then when you get looking into things more, I mean, the first place we wrote an offer on didn't even happen at the end of the day...

(Justin):   *"That was the first place in the Southside..."*

(G): Yeah, that's right. It had a suite in the basement but it wasn't legal. And then you put the fear of God into me about the legalities of having a suite that didn't have proper development permits, and the ramifications of that...That was an eye opener. So when we looked at finding a house that was lower-priced, that I could make INTO a property with a legal suite in the basement, it was going to cost more money to undo what someone had incorrectly done than for me to just find a better-priced property and take the project on myself.

So when we went back after the inspection on the first place and said "Well, to rectify these deficiencies, we need to take '$XXXXX' off the price" and they basically told us to take a flying leap...

(Justin): *"Yeah, 'Leap' was the F-word they definitely used..."*

(G): Hahaha, right! So we walked from that and bought Property #1, which was good because it had a partially finished basement but I could quickly demolish that and start with a blank slate. And we took action on that place because at the time, the acreage hadn't sold yet.

And then when the acreage sold, now it was like 'ok, time to buy another property...' and I was already in the middle of the first basement conversion to a legal suite so I thought "Alright, let's just do this" and we started the second project on Property #2. And at the time, I was renting out the top suite on Property #1 so I couldn't move in there, so we got Property #2, I moved in upstairs, and then was managing two basement suite projects concurrently.

And the discussion around the locations for both properties really revolved around "What's the DIRT worth?" As you like to say. ie. What areas of the city command good rents relative to the price of entry into owning a home in that area, and that also have high demand for rental accommodations that tenants are looking for.

(Justin): *"Oh yeah, I forgot you had immediately rented the top suite out on Property #1! So you really did need to buy Property #2 after the acreage sold otherwise you'd have been renting or homeless!"*

(G): Uh huh! Lol. And it worked out good because having the instant income at Property #1 was great, because it basically took care of the expenses of Property #1 while I invested in the basement suite conversion. And then the real cashflow would start once the suite was finished and rented out.

Then we talked about the government grants (cornerstone program)...but you could only get a maximum of I think $25k at the time?

(Justin): *"And there were some limiting factors on how much you could charge for rent to prospective tenants."*

(G): Right, and it wasn't as ideal a scenario so I figured "Why bother with the government funds if it's going to limit my upside and total cashflow potential?"

(Justin): *"That's correct. They were saying you could only rent to median-income tenants, and that "median" was determined of course by the City that was handing you the grant money, and those figures were very low compared to actual real-market rents..."*

(G): Right, and I'm all about maximizing my return.

(Justin): *"Precisely! You're a pragmatist!"*

(G): So that was how all that kinda went. I tho~~ugh~~ "Let's just give it a go" and made myself a Contractor on two projects at once.

(Justin): *Are you okay with sharing relative numbers, roughly? Like, with Property #1...ok, backing the train up here a bit, you've got Property #1, it has a tenant in the suite upstairs (a 3 BR 1 BA main floor suite), you've built out a 2 BR 1 BA basement suite, and this place is in a great neighbourhood...And then you've got Property #2 in a REALLY great neighbourhood, and you paid significantly more to acquire that property because of the location, but you also had higher rental potential because of the even more-desirable location...What does that look like?"* (Ed: *At the time of publication, we are referencing about 2-3 years previous*).

(G): Ok, so back then, I was getting, because the rents were a bit higher, I was getting 11-12% cash-on-cash return? (Ed: *positive cashflow, divided by how much downpayment+renovation costs+closing costs were invested into the property. In the case of Property #1, this was roughly $130,000 between downpayment, renovation costs, and closing costs*). And this wasn't including factoring in any mortgage-reduction, which brings the total closer to 18-20% return. And then on the place I was living in, Property #2, I was in the upstairs suite myself, and renting out the new basement suite, but when you consider I invested more into that basement suite conversion than the first property…

(Justin): *"Right, I forgot about that. Heated floors, all day…"*

(G): It was ONLY in the bathrooms!!

(Justin): *"Hahahaha!"*

(*Ed: G.Yeezy had asked me once whether she should spend $2k "steamrolling" the gravel driveway at property #2 as a courtesy to his brand new tenant, to which I scolded him and asked what the tires on their vehicles were going to do for him, for free…So the running joke was that "steamroller" money was investing in frivolous things that don't provide an immediate ROI/Return-On-Investment…Heated floors was a luxury she added to BOTH the upstairs and downstairs bathrooms on Property #2…Which I consistently give him a hard time about to this day…*).

(G): Heated floors are NOT steamroller money…

(Justin): *"No, no. You're right. I have to admit, I've shown a lot of places lately to a recent client who comes from a warmer climate, and that was his whiny demand, and I give him a hard time about it but truthfully I'm sold on heated floors. You did good. It's a good thing. SO back to the Numbers…"*

(G): Thanks! So Property #2, that was running around 9%, when I factored in the cost of additional renovations to that suite.

(Justin): *"And, I'm recalling a brief conversation here, a few years ago, and shortly after you had gotten both projects finished and all three Rental units rented out with tenants and you were living upstairs at Property #2, so you went from a three-quarter of a million dollar acreage, that you're paying ALL the expenses for out of your own income...To owning, at the time, and values have fluctuated a little bit over the years now, and the interesting thing is because of WHERE we got these places for you, the values have gone down a touch, but not significantly, and with the economy softening and the rental market softening, rents have gone down a touch as well, but not significantly, and that mostly has to do with the dirt that you bought, ie. the desirable LOCATIONS you invest in...."*

(G): Yeah, with the shift in the economy over the last few years, Property #1 is down to maybe an 8% return, and property #2 is at about a 7% return, again, not factoring in principal reduction on my mortgages...

(Justin): *"Ok, but you basically went from that big acreage, paying all the bills... to now owning just under $1million dollars of real estate between properties #1 & 2, and I remember you telling me, based on the positive cashflow from property #1, the* *upstairs and downstairs being fully rented out, how much cashflow that spun off that you then used to cover your own costs of living at property #2, let alone with that property's basement suite being rented out as well and collecting that revenue, you went from roughly spending a few thousand a month on one property in the $750k range to now owning nearly $1million dollars of real estate, and it only costing you $500 out-of-pocket when you calculated all the positive cashflow..."*

(G): Yeah, give or take, that's about right.

(Justin): *"And the beauty is that it's ALL paid by someone else..."*

(G): Yup. That's pretty much about right, haha...

(Justin): *"Man, I love that! So what are some of the challenges you didn't maybe expect, in terms of being an owner/landlord and living upstairs and having someone live downstairs, as was the case on property #2....And by extension, the other things you've learned with Property #1 being fully rented out as well..."*

(G): For sure. You definitely learn to be handy really quick. If I could fix something basic on my own instead of spending $80 or $100/hr on a tradesperson to do it, when it was something simple, I learned really quick how to take care of the minor things. The major things obviously I call a qualified professional to deal with. What else... A lot of it was learning about setting the expectations right from the get-go, with the RIGHT tenants. And before we sat down here to record, Sandy and I were talking about this...we were just saying, you've got this process of identifying renters, and you've helped me with that quite a bit with your "Flaming Hoops" strategy...but identifying renters, and using the interviewing skills I've previously gained from my past job, it was for me about determining whether or not somebody I was looking to rent to, whether they would truly care about the place they were going to rent from me. It's about having your process, and being disciplined enough to follow it and not make exceptions. I mean, you remember all the times I would text you asking "Ahhh, man, do I do it? Do I not do it? Do I rent to these people or not?" And it was just kinda like "No, stick with it, you'll find the RIGHT people..."

(Justin): *"So true!"*

(G): My first tenant, where I lived... The "banana boy"... at Property #2, my basement tenant... he was a yoga instructor, he had just moved out on his own, and I remember him and his roommate having a huge argument and I remember hearing them from upstairs and I was just thinking like "Shut up already, it's 2am..." but they had JUST moved out from mom and dads, and this was their first place on their own, so they didn't really have a respect for the fact they had someone else living upstairs just yet...

(Justin): *"Well, some people just aren't "Grade-A" students now are they?"*

(G): Hahaha, yes. So they broke their lease, and I was okay with that because I wanted them out anyways, and they were trying to renegotiate their lease...

(Justin): *"Yeah, no."*

(G): Exactly. No way, right? So there are those kinds of things. There's always going to be stories about tenants, negative ones, but at the same time, we've mostly had really great tenants.

Like, one of our current tenants, the other day, she made us cookies and gave them to us for Christmas. Fresh-baked!

(Justin): *"Man, you're lucky! My tenant never gives me anything like that. Not that I'd trust his baking anyways...hahaha (Kevin, if you read this, I love you man!). But he's awesome and he always pays on-time so I can't ask for more than that."*

(G): What else... Handyman stuff. It's good to have a network of just-in-case contacts. The "I Got A Guy" sort of list.

(Justin): *" "I got a guy!" That's right! You're like a walking Rolodex of contacts like that..."*

(G): Pretty much! And you've got to keep on top of filling that list because tradespeople come and go. And sometimes good ones turn out to not be so good long term. So you've got to be on the lookout for others to fill those spots on your go-to list.

(Justin): *"Great advice."*

(G): And you've also got to know where to get things like appliances and supplies for better-than-retail pricing. Like, appliances, I've got a few sources for scratch-and-dent outlets for example.

(Justin): *"Because you 'got-a-guy!' "*

(G): Now, some people talk about negligent landlords as 'slum-landlords', and in my previous industry in financial services, for our clientele, we weren't always the lowest-cost service provider because we provided a lot of extra certainty and value than our lower-priced competitors. And so I've applied that philosophy to how I do my rentals, because my aim is NOT to be the lowest-priced rental option. And people sometimes try to negotiate a lower rate, but I tell them "Look, if you want to pay THAT price, that's fine. But not for the quality and care that I provide to my tenants."

I always tell people I'm like the SONY product versus the cheap in-house brand at say Future Shop...

(Justin): *"Not sure if you can use that analogy*

anymore given where Future Shop is at nowadays!"

(G): True, true. But you get what I'm saying. And that proves my point. That competing on lowest-price only puts you in a position where you don't have the higher margin and ability to really deliver a great product and great experience to your customers, or in the case of rentals, your tenants.

And so what I was telling Sandy earlier, that if you want to sign a tenant more than your tenant wants to sign with you, that's a recipe for compromise and it's not a good way to start a business relationship long-term with that tenant. If I want the tenant more than they want my place, not a good thing.

That's something that is difficult to stay disciplined on, especially if you're not getting a lot of bites on your rental ads when you've got a vacancy for one of your units. You've got to have patience.

(Justin): *"Great points G. And I guess patience is one thing, but being patient while your going broke isn't a viable strategy long-term just to secure a "good" tenant. So on the topic of being in a position where you can afford to wait for the right tenant, how do you personally mitigate that potential for loss from vacancy, so you can be disciplined and stick to your guns instead of chasing and signing a low-quality tenant just to fill a vacancy?"*

(G): Well, this kind of ties into my financial services training. And one of the pillars is that yo have to have a savings fund. You need to be able to manage at least 2 months of costs, at a bare minimum, without a renter in your unit. Obviously that's not ideal. But you can't be living month-to-month and needing that income to cover your costs that month. In your own personal finances, if you yourself are living month-to-month and you're one missed paycheque away from not paying all your bills, then you shouldn't be getting into this game at all. Because it's just going to magnify your stress that much more.

That would be my personal take on it. So that'd be one thing, having savings. The other thing would be, having that process of "Ok, somebody wants to rent my unit, can I turn it around in a snap?" Ie. Do I have my rental agreements ready to go. I went from being mostly paper-based, to now like what you guys do at EMPOWER, with electronic signatures and things like emailing signed documents immediately to tenants etc.

My time share rentals are done that way. Our property rentals are like that now. I can send documents out asap, tenants can sign and get it done and back to me with a few clicks, and it's all ready to go. And paying rent, they can obviously set up e-transfers and such. Granted, cash is still an acceptable form of legal tender!

(Justin): *"Always will be! Hahaha!"*

(G): Of course! I mean, at one point I was receiving a combination of e-transfers, I was getting cash from these two young guys that were mechanics that were renting the basement suite out at property #1, I was getting post-dated cheques, certified cheques...

(Justin): *"You get any money orders yet?"*

(G): Yes! I did get one of those once. I had one tenant where, we had agreed, if the cheque bounced even once, from then on it was cash or money order or bank draft, and he gave me money orders.

(Justin): *"You know you're a legit landlord/investor when you've accepted a money order for payment of back-rent!"*

(G): Absolutely. And so, those would be the main things. And of course, taking care of your property. I also subscribe to the philosophy of "I'm going to zero-ground this, so I know where the baseline is". And if yo think about financial management or anything like that, or even like with condominiums, right? You've got reserve fund studies. Reports that show you where you have to have things replaced or repaired in a certain lifespan or time frame. And I use that same philosophy on my rental properties. You may not do that with your own personal residence, and may differ maintenance costs or upgrades because you have that autonomy, but with my rentals, I make sure to keep on top of those things so the costs don't eventually spiral out of control.

You need to be responsible that way. And besides, they're all deductions anyways! You've got to look at things from the perspective of. "Investment" versus "Expense". With your rentals, when you're spending money on maintaining and upgrading things, they're an investment that protects your revenue stream. Having that "business builder" mindset is saying "Yes, obviously there's expenses. But many of those items are truly investments in maintaining your asset for the long-term". So you need to look at things that way.

Long-term, it'll maintain and increase the value of your asset. And at the end of the day, guess what, it's gotta be done. And a gain, it's a write-off. If you do things yourself, you've got to figure out is it really worth your time or should you be hiring a pro and spending your time making a better return on your time in your main business or your main job. Plus, if you hire yourself and pay yourself to do a task, you can't write that off, right?

(Justin): *"What would you do differently, knowing what you know now?"*

(G): What would I do differently? I think now that we've gone from these two properties, to what we have now, and the two most recent being a townhouse purchase and also another home with a suite that was already built into the basement, I think I'd rather focus on buying homes that have suite-potential and taking that on myself instead of going for a place where the work is already done.

(Justin): *"Something that's got the good bones...."*

(G): That's right. Because then I know what I've got and I'm not constantly second-guessing what someone else did. And also, I've reduced my level of patience when it comes to evicting tenants that aren't pulling their end of the bargain.

In the past I've been too lenient and now, I make sure that the line is clearly draw and when it's crossed, we take the appropriate legal action to protect our investment and remove a non-paying tenant. And I say legal because in the past, when we had one tenant that had fallen far behind on payment, we found out that there's a certain process that we have to follow to legally serve that eviction notice, versus simply posting it on a tenant's door.

You've got to start the court process at the same time as serving the notice so that way you're not dragging things on and wasting time and incurring another extra month or two of non-payment from a renter who's playing the system. You can always cancel a court-date, but if you wait to take that action, it could cost you needlessly.

(Justin): *"More solid advice."*

(G): And then in terms of the type of property I'm looking for now, at this stage of the game, triplexes, fourplexes...

(Justin): *"Small villages in Eastern European countries..."*

(G): Hahaha, right. But really, we're looking at scale. And also looking at building, from the ground up, a purpose-built multi-family rental property. And that takes a lot of connections in order to be a successful builder, right?

(Justin): *"That's really awesome, G. So, you've really progressed beyond just those two properties now. Are you ok talking about how your #HouseHack has gotten you to this point where you're at now, and what that looks like? And would you have gotten here without the #HouseHack?"*

(G): Yeah, for sure we can talk about that. It's lead to getting two more properties: the townhouse rental, and then another place with a rental suite, that I currently live in and rent the basement suite out. And Property #2 is now fully rented with tenants up and down. Definitely wouldn't have been able to get to this stage, that's for sure. And honestly, I might have just bought another vacation property..

(Justin): *"And paid for the costs all out of pocket..."*

(G): Exactly!

(Justin): *"Yurt's on the beach in Kona are always still an option..."*

(G): I definitely look at real estate differently than I did before though.

(Justin): *"Well, I very much appreciate you taking the time to have this chat. Especially given that your base-level of #HouseHack and real estate experience is really on the top end of the ladder for what a lot of people reading this book are going to be aiming for in their own lives. But your story gives a sense of perspective about the possibilities that you can really take this #HouseHack concept to, if yo want to go beyond just owning one place and utilizing the spare space to create income."*

(G): Absolutely. It's yet a matter of scale. When I started, it was about going from one property to two. And then going beyond that and asking "How can I grow this and scale this?"

And anybody can do it, they just need to decide and take the next step. Go bigger on the next step. It's definitely not get-rich-quick. If you can't balance your own budget, or you think this is going to make you super-wealthy overnight, this isn't the right thing for you.

(Justin): *"Totally makes sense. Give your head a shake if you think that, eh?"*

(G): Totally. This is a buy-and-hold strategy.

(Justin): *"Right. I mean, I liken it to 'planting oak-seeds'. You're not going to plant a seed today and* *have a huge oak tree tomorrow. But long-term..."*

(G): Totally. It's all about long-term thinking.

(Justin): *"Also, and this is going into the book, but I wanted to point out the socks that you're wearing today, and that they've got penguins on them. And I think they're great. So I'm going to take a picture and put that in the book, ok?"*

(G): That's right! My socks. Ok, sounds good. I also have other ones that say "I don't have to be good, I'm cute".

(Justin): *"Hahaha, you need to wear those next time! Or stick with your regular white crew socks..."*

(G): Yes, with my very-white running shoes. So I can look like an old man...

(Justin): *"You're an old soul at heart. I love it. And so you're okay with sharing your story and comments for the book? And do you want a pseudonym?"*

(G): For sure. How's 'Sweet Potato'?

(Justin): *"What?? Lol. How about 'G. Yeezy??' "*

(G): Sure, that sounds fun!

(Justin): *"Ok, done!"*

G. Yeezy's House Hack Summary:

Property Types:

•1950's/1960's era Bungalows Off Whyte Ave (x2) with Legal Basement Suites

•Principal Residence - 1960's era Bungalow in Southside with Basement Suite

•Townhouse in West Edmonton

Previous Property:
Worth Approx. $750k, @$0 Income

Post #HouseHack:
FOUR Properties Worth Approx. $1.6 Million +/-, @$6-Figures Gross Annual Rents

*G.Yeezy's initial #HouseHack involved her first two places, then picking up the rental townhouse, and then what is now a principal residence with suite. The first two places had a valuation of approx. $900k+ after renovating and installing basement suites. Total portfolio value is now around $1.6m at the time of publication. This took less than five years to accomplish…

"SO WHAT'S NEXT?"

That all depends on your, Dear Reader.

If you're reading this, you likely fall into one of a few possible categories:

1) You're a first-time home buyer in the Edmonton, AB region and you saw our book on the shelves of Chapters, Audrey's Books on Jasper Ave, or you clicked on a Facebook promotion or heard about EMPOWER Real Estate Group and/or this book from a friend of yours who's part of the EMPOWER Family already.

2) You're not a first-time buyer, but you're interested in making real estate work for you instead of paying for all property related expenses on your own. Perhaps you're open to taking advantage of a room mate #HouseHack scenario…Or maybe you've got the means and determination to find a place with a secondary suite that's separate from your living space.

3) Third is, you're seeing our marketing material for this book and you reside outside the Edmonton, AB region but you're curious about the #HouseHack concept and want to know if there are like-minded real estate professionals, mortgage brokers or loan officers, etc. in your area that you can rely on to help you get into your own #HouseHack strategy.

If you're in the last category, I'd invite you to visit **Consult.HouseHackBook.com** and pass your details on. We can potentially put you in touch with client-focused, non-pushy real estate professionals to assist you with your #HouseHack home search.

If you're in the second or first categories, then I've invite you to reach out directly. Either email us at:

Justin@EmpowerRealEstateGroup.com

or Call/Text direct @ **780-405-5272** for fastest response and schedule your Initial Consultation today.

"But I'm not quite ready!"

That's fine. PREPARATION is key to success. Even if you're 6 months, or even 12+ months away from being in a position to make a move, we consistently find that those who reach out ahead of time and keep connected are the clients who end up achieving their goals in smooth fashion. Because they're PREPARED.

In fact, our most successful clients are the ones who DON'T rush into home-buying decisions.

Planning, Being Prepared, and following a Proven Process....These are the things that give you Clarity.

And Clarity inevitably leads to better decisions.

If you're looking for pushy real estate agent to help you with your next move, EMPOWER isn't going to be a good fit for you.

But if you desire expertise and dedication to client-results, coupled with laid back personalities (that absolutely get aggressive during negotiations on your behalf!), then EMPOWER might be what you're looking for in a real estate professional.

Schedule your Initial Consultation and let's see if we're a good fit to work together to reach your real estate goals and start your #HouseHack journey!

"What if I'm ready to go, right now!?"

Again, we're not here to rush buyers into real estate decisions. All our client relationships start with an Initial Consultation. But if you're like Travis L. (see his story earlier in the book, on page 28-29), there's no reason why the Process needs to take months when it can take mere weeks to get the ball rolling (provided the right property shows up on the market for you).

Either email us at:

Justin@EmpowerRealEstateGroup.com

or Call/Text direct @ **780-405-5272** for fastest response and schedule your Initial Consultation today.

Regardless of whether or not your plans involve us connecting in-person sooner or later, I wish you, Dear Reader, nothing but the best success with your real estate goals, and in your life!

-Justin La Favor

RESOURCES

If you happen to live in the Edmonton, AB / Capital Region and want to start your #HouseHack journey right (or even if you've read the book and decided #HouseHacking isn't for you BUT you're still interested in finding your first or next home), here are some helpful professionals we deal with on a regular basis.

Per RECA (Real Estate Council of Alberta) guidelines, we are obligated to disclose any referral fee or compensation we receive by referring other professionals or services....And we don't get a dime, in this case.

The reason we can confidently vouch for the professionals listed below is because we've either had them work with/for us personally on both co-authors' personal real estate transactions, or we've had the pleasure of working with them on deals for other clients in the EMPOWER Family over the years.

We refer them because we know them, we like them, we trust them, and because they'll love our clients and treat them like family.

With that, turn the page for contact details of Preferred Professionals in the EMPOWER Family...

FINANCING / MORTGAGE SPECIALISTS

Shayne Beeler - OneSt Mortgages (Edmonton)
780-700-7787 // shayneb@onest.ca **www.OneSt.ca**
• Also has partners and office in Saskatoon, SK in case you have family/friends that unfortunately cheer for the Riders… ;-)

Karine Perin - BMO (Terwillegar Branch)
780-408-0847 // karine.perin@bmo.com

www.MortgageSistersWest.ca
Danielle Franke & Nadia DeVenz
780-237-1730 (Dani) // 780-660-4654 (Nadia)
danielle@MortgageSistersWest.ca
nadia@MortgageSistersWest.ca
River City Financial - Mortgage Architects

Louis Nguyen - ATB (Jasper Place Branch)
780-392-7107 // lnguyen@atb.com

LAWYERS

Ralph Colistro - Colistro Law (Edmonton)
780-800-0484 // ralph@Colistro.ca **www.Colistro.ca**

Violeta Boquiren - Boquiren Law (Edmonton)
780-484-2453 // vgbkerr@gmail.com

Kathy Tarrabain - Raponi Rideout Tarrabain
780-486-8686 // kathy@tarrabain.net

INSPECTORS

Brent Podruzny / Kyle Dowdeswell
A Buyer's Choice Inspections
780-221-3569 (Brent) // 780-224-1151 (Kyle)
brent.podruzny@abuyerschoice.com

Randy Murray - A Closer Look Inspections
780-906-5335 // randy@ACloserLookInspections.ca
www.ACloserLookInspections.ca

Steve Pentyliuk - Technologic Inspections Inc.
780-499-7672 // scoutersteve@shaw.ca
www.TechnologicInspections.com

We have a number of other specialized contacts in the trades industries to help you get acquainted with potential costs to fix items that may arise during a home inspection, or to help you gain perspective on the level of investment a given property may require to install a legal basement suite. Don't hesitate to reach out for referrals... We're never too busy to promote great trades people!

HAVE A FRIEND THAT'S LOOKING TO BUY (OR SELL)?

Lots of agents talk about how "referrals are the highest compliment I can receive". And while it's become somewhat of a cliche, there's a reason…

Cliches typically have a lot of truth to them.

And there's no greater level of trust than for one individual to say to another "You need to check these folks out, here's why I trust them and why you should to…"

So if you resonate with the messages we've shared in this book, or perhaps you've Googled us or looked us up on social media, and you like how we serve our clients….

…We're never too busy to serve someone from your circle of influence. If you'd like to pass our name on to someone, you want a handful of business cards to keep handy, or maybe even a spare copy of this very book to give away, we'd be happy to oblige. Just go to the following website and jot down your request…

(See next page…)

www.ReferAFriendToJustin.com

or touch base with Sandy directly by visiting...

www.ReferAFriendToSandy.com

Thanks in advance for keeping us in mind when someone you know of is looking for Clarity with their real estate goals!

WANT TO SEARCH FOR LISTINGS WITH ZERO STRINGS ATTACHED?

(And we'll share a little-known secret why realtor.ca is NOT the best website to search for new listings. More on that below...)

What most people don't know is that realtor.ca is NOT the actual MLS® system. It's actually the local real estate board's database that is the "Brains" of the local MLS® system.

The realtor.ca website, and the term MLS® are trademarks of the Canadian Real Estate Association (CREA). This is the national association that all REALTOR®s are members of, in addition to their provincial and local associations. As such, the property info you see on this website is merely the public access point for all the local board's databases.

Which means.... It can take up to 24+ hours for a new listing to show up on that public website! Not only that, but if it's a hot listing, not only have all the sharp local agents seen it already...But their clients that are signed up on a website that is tied into the LOCAL BOARD DATABASE will also have seen it too via direct searches or instant email notifications.

In short…

If you want to miss out on the hottest new listings and let other buyers beat you to the punch, then continue using realtor.ca!

But…

If you want the same fast access to virtually all the data that we see as agents, on the local board database, then you should sign up at our home-search website:

www.YourHassleFreeHomeSearch.com

There's no spam, no auto-responder email series you'll be automatically signed up for, none of that BS.

It's a 100% No Hassle, No Obligation, No Pushy-Sales-Tactics home search experience…Guaranteed!

(This website is for use by those intending to view property listed on the REALTOR®s Association of Edmonton database. If you're in another city/area, visit **consult.HouseHackBook.com** and type in your details and we'll see if we can match you with a qualified real estate professional in your area.)

ON SOCIAL MEDIA? LET'S CONNECT!

(You're missing out on all the epic videos and content we drop if you're not on our social media channels…Don't miss out!)

Facebook:
www.Facebook.com/EmpowerRealEstateGroup

YouTube:
Search -> "Empower Real Estate Group"

Instagram:
Justin La Favor -> @mrlafavor
Sandy Umrysh -> @sandyumrysh

#HouseHack

Made in the USA
Columbia, SC
24 June 2018